FOR MEN ONLY:
MASTERING THE MICROWAVE

FOR MEN ONLY:
MASTERING THE MICROWAVE

by
CiCi Williamson
and
John A. Kelly

BARRON'S

Woodbury, New York • London • Toronto • Sydney

All inquiries should be addressed to:

Barron's Educational Series, Inc.
113 Crossways Park Drive
Woodbury, New York 11797

International Standard Book No. 0-8120-5704-X

Library of Congress Catalog Card No. 86-3410

Library of Congress Cataloging-in-Publication Data
Williamson, Cici.
    For men only: mastering the microwave

    Includes index.
    1. Microwave cookery.   I. Kelly, John A.   II. Title.
III. Series.
TX832.W55   1986   641.5'882   86-3410
ISBN 0-8120-5704-X

PRINTED IN JAPAN

6 7 8 9   9 8 7 6 5 4 3 2 1

Credits
Color photographs: Matthew Klein
Food Stylist: Andrea Swenson
Prop Stylist: Linda Cheverton
Line Art: Frank Senyk

Cover
Milton Glaser, Inc.

CONTENTS

COOKING NOTES

KITCHEN TIPS

All spoon measures are level unless otherwise stated. All fruits and vegetables are medium size unless indicated. All other information regarding ingredients and preparations are included in the recipes. For additional information, see Index.

The following are conversion tables and tips for cooks in Australia, Canada, and Great Britain. The cup and spoon measures in this book are U.S. Customary (cup = 236 mL; tablespoon = 15 mL). Use these tables when working with British Imperial or metric kitchen utensils.

KEY TO SYMBOLS

`1.00*` Indicates minimum preparation and cooking times in hours and minutes. They do not include prepared items in the list of ingredients; calculated times apply only to the method. An asterisk * indicates extra time should be allowed, so check the note below symbols.

Chef's hats indicate degree of difficulty of a recipe: no hat means it is straightforward; one hat slightly more complicated; two hats indicates it is for more advanced cooks.

$ Indicates a recipe which is good value for money; $$ indicates an expensive recipe. No $ sign indicates an inexpensive recipe.

✳ Indicates that a recipe will freeze. If there is no symbol, the recipe is unsuitable for freezing. An asterisk * indicates special freezer instructions, so check the note immediately below the symbols.

`309 cals` Indicates calories per serving, including any serving suggestions (for example, cream, to serve) given in the list of ingredients.

SOLID MEASURES

For cooks measuring items by weight, here are approximate equivalents, in both Imperial and metric. So as to avoid awkward measurements, some conversions are not exact.

	U.S. CUSTOMARY	METRIC	IMPERIAL
Butter	1 cup	225 g	8 oz
	1/2 cup	115 g	4 oz
	1/4 cup	60 g	2 oz
	1 Tbsp	15 g	1/2 oz
Cheese (grated)	1 cup	115 g	4 oz
Fruit (chopped fresh)	1 cup	225 g	8 oz
Herbs (chopped fresh)	1/4 cup	7 g	1/4 oz
Meats/Chicken (chopped, cooked)	1 cup	175 g	6 oz
Mushrooms (chopped, fresh)	1 cup	70 g	2 1/2 oz
Nuts (chopped)	1 cup	115 g	4 oz
Raisins (and other dried chopped fruits)	1 cup	175 g	6 oz
Rice (uncooked)	1 cup	225 g	8 oz
(cooked)	3 cups	225 g	8 oz
Vegetables (chopped, raw)	1 cup	115 g	4 oz

LIQUID MEASURES

The Imperial pint is larger than the U.S. pint; therefore, note the following when measuring liquid ingredients.

U.S.	IMPERIAL
1 cup = 8 fluid ounces	1 cup = 10 fluid ounces
1/2 cup = 4 fluid ounces	1/2 cup = 5 fluid ounces
1 tablespoon = 3/4 fluid ounce	1 tablespoon = 1 fluid ounce

U.S. MEASURE	METRIC APPROXIMATE	IMPERIAL APPROXIMATE
1 quart (4 cups)	950 mL	1 1/2 pints + 4 Tbsp
1 pint (2 cups)	450 mL	3/4 pint
1 cup	236 mL	1/4 pint + 6 Tbsp
1 Tbsp	15 mL	1+ Tbsp
1 tsp	5mL	1 tsp

DRY MEASURES

Outside the United States, the following items are measured by weight. Use the following table, but bear in mind that measurements will vary, depending on the variety of flour and moisture. Cup measurements are loosely packed; flour is measured directly from package (presifted).

	U.S. CUSTOMARY	METRIC	IMPERIAL
Flour (all-purpose)	1 cup	150 g	5 oz
Cornmeal	1 cup	175 g	6 oz
Sugar (granulated)	1 cup	190 g	6 1/2 oz
(confectioners)	1 cup	80 g	2 2/3 oz
(brown)	1 cup	160 g	5 1/3 oz

OVEN TEMPERATURES

Fahrenheit	225	300	350	400	450
Celsius	110	150	180	200	230
Gas Mark	1/4	2	4	6	8

(conversion information continues on page 160)

INTRODUCTION

If a man doesn't know how to cook, it's not because cooking is difficult. Some of the world's greatest chefs are men. A non-cooking man either has always had someone doing it for him, or is just not interested in learning.

Cooking is fun! It is one of the creative activities in "keeping house." Whether as husbands, bachelors, widowers, or divorcés, more men than ever enjoy feeding themselves and others. And this book is our attempt to interest even more men in cooking, and to make learning how to cook easier. A microwave oven is the perfect appliance for a busy man to use, because it cooks fast and makes cleaning up easy. Perhaps this is the reason why almost half the microwave ovens sold today are purchased by men.

Nothing is more appealing to most women than having a man in the kitchen. Since women usually do most of the cooking, it is a special treat to have a man take over and prepare something delicious. If a woman has given you this book, that's a big hint!

Whether you're reading this book to survive, enjoy, or impress, we hope you will find what we have written helpful, informative, and fun. If you already know how to cook, you will find some new and useful ideas. If you have never cooked, we have written the directions clearly enough that you can make the most difficult recipe your first time.

The recipes in this book were developed for use in ovens producing between 600 and 700 watts. If you have a "compact" microwave oven with 500 watts of cooking power, you will need to add 1/4 to 1/3 extra time than is specified in the recipe. The power levels used in the recipes are explained on page 131.

The word *microwave* can have several meanings: as an appliance, a radio wave, or a cooking procedure. Throughout these recipes, we've used it in abbreviated form **(MW)** as a verb meaning, "to cook in the microwave oven." For example, the recipe might say, **"MW on high** for 1 minute."

Instructions for rotating the dishes have been given in an effort to ensure that foods will cook evenly in approximately 40 different brands of microwave ovens. If your oven has a rotating food turntable, no other rotating is required. However, you must stir the food or turn the food upside down as the recipe instructs.

If a food should be loosely covered with a lid, plastic wrap, waxed paper, or paper towels, the recipe will so state. If the recipe does not say to cover the food, do not cover it.

Teasers

The microwave oven is a host's best friend. You can prepare and arrange appetizers ahead of time on microwave-save serving dishes. If the time required for reheating each dish is noted on a piece of paper nearby, you can quickly microwave the foods when the guests arrive. Be prepared for unexpected guests by keeping useful ingredients in your pantry and have previously cooked teasers in the freezer. Thaw and heat them in a flash, and serve them to your hungry guests.

LUCKY NEW YEAR'S DIP

| 0.10 | ✳ | 409 cals |

Yields 1 qt

2 slices bacon, diced

2 cans (16 oz) black-eyed peas

1 tsp instant minced onion

1 can (4 oz) chopped green chiles

½ cup shredded Cheddar cheese

sliced green onions for garnish

1 Place bacon in a 1-qt casserole. Cover and **MW on high** for 3 minutes, or until bacon is desired doneness.

2 Drain peas, reserving ¼ cup liquid. Put peas and liquid into food processor or blender and puree. Add to bacon and drippings in casserole. Stir in minced onion and undrained chiles. Top with cheese and garnish with green onions. **MW on 70% (medium-high)** for 5 to 6 minutes, or until dip is hot and cheese is melted. Serve with tortilla chips.

NEW YEAR'S DAY
Southerners believe that in order to have good luck during the coming year, you must eat some black-eyed peas on January 1. Instead of eating yours as a vegetable, try our dip, made from pureed peas.

STAN SMITH'S NACHOS

| 0.03 | 97 cals |

Serves 4 to 6

1 bag (8 oz) round tortilla chips

1 can (16 oz) refried beans with sausage

1 cup shredded Cheddar cheese

slices of jalapeño pepper

1 Make as many batches of nachos as you want until the ingredients run out! For one batch of nachos, put 10 tortilla chips on a microwave-safe plate. Place about 2 tsp of refried beans on each chip and sprinkle with some cheese. Top each chip with a slice of jalapeño pepper.

2 Turning plate halfway around after 30 seconds, **MW on high** for 1 minute, or until cheese melts and nachos are hot. Repeat for additional batches.

NOTE
Stan Smith is a world famous tennis player. Stan loves to fix these nachos in the microwave.

STALE CHIPS

If you have some chips or crackers that have gone stale, you can freshen them in the microwave oven. Put 2 paper towels on the floor of your oven. Spread a layer of chips or crackers on top of the paper towels. Cover with another paper towel. **MW on high** for 30 to 60 seconds, depending upon quantity. Remove from oven, uncover, and let chips or crackers stand. They will become crisp again as they cool.

BRANDIED CHICKEN LIVER PÂTÉ

| 0.10 | ✳ | 135 cals |

Serves 4

8 oz chicken livers

1/2 cup water

2 green onions, cut into 1-in pieces

2 Tbsp butter or margarine

4 tsp brandy

salt, ground nutmeg, and black pepper to taste

assorted crackers

1 Wash livers and place in a 4-cup glass measure. Add water and cover with plastic wrap. **MW on high** for 4 to 5 minutes, or until livers are no longer pink. Pour off water and discard.

2 Place cooked livers in a blender or food processor with steel blade. Add onions, butter, and brandy. Process until livers are smooth.

3 Add salt, nutmeg, and pepper to taste; pulse mixture briefly. Pack mixture into an 8-oz ramekin or small ceramic pot; chill, then serve with assorted crackers.

FOR LIVER LOVERS

Chicken livers are usually packaged in cartons. They can be frozen in the carton for up to 6 months. To thaw livers in the microwave, remove the lid and put the carton in the oven. **MW on 30% (medium-low)** for 5 to 7 minutes per pound.

After half the cooking time, remove livers from carton and place in a glass measuring cup. Separate livers as soon as they thaw, and rinse under cool water, then pat dry.

Livers sometimes make a popping sound when microwaved. No worry, but keep the utensil covered.

JOE PATERNO'S ANTIPASTO

| 0.35 | 🍴 | 200 cals |

Yields 2 qt

2 medium carrots, peeled and sliced into coins

4 Tbsp olive oil

1 large onion, chopped

5 ribs celery, sliced

½ head fresh cauliflower, cut into flowerets

8 oz fresh mushrooms, sliced

1 large green bell pepper, sliced

1 bottle (14 oz) ketchup

1 bottle (12 oz) chili sauce

1½ tsp salt

1 tsp MSG (optional)

1 clove garlic, minced

juice of 1 lemon

1 can (6 oz) tuna, drained

1 lb frozen king crab meat, thawed and drained (optional)

1 jar (6 oz) marinated artichoke hearts, including liquid

¼ cup sliced green olives

¼ cup sliced black olives

1 Place carrots and olive oil in a 4-qt pot. Cover and **MW on high** for 3 minutes. Add onion and celery. Cover and **MW on high** for 2 minutes. Add cauliflower. Cover and **MW on high** for 2 minutes. Add mushrooms and bell pepper. Cover and **MW on high** for 2 minutes. Set aside.

2 In a 2-qt glass bowl, mix ketchup, chili sauce, salt, MSG, garlic, and lemon juice. Break up tuna and crab meat and add to sauce. Add artichoke hearts, including liquid, then add olives. Pour mixture into pot with cooked vegetables. Mix, then cover and let marinate in refrigerator for at least 24 hours. This antipasto will stay fresh for a week.

Serving Suggestion
Antipasto is typically served cold. Arrange romaine lettuce leaves on a round tray and spoon the desired amount of antipasto into the center. But this vegetable salad can also be served as a first course at dinner or as a salad for lunch. It may also be served hot; reheat in microwave on high until it is serving temperature.

NOTE
The original recipe given to us by Coach Paterno was sufficient to feed the entire Penn State University football team! We've reduced it for easier microwaving.

CHEF'S CLASS

Albacore tuna yields the whitest meat and is the most expensive variety. The majority of tuna consumed is "light meat" form — the yellowfin, skipjack, and bluefin tuna. Canned tuna that is packed in water has very few calories — 127 for a 3½-oz s⁻ ng. Tuna packed in oil has more than twice that number of calories.

When you open a jar or can of olives, remove the olives

you need and leave the rest in their liquid. Transfer canned olives with liquid into a glass jar with a screw top. Store all olives in the refrigerator for up to 1 month; the heavily brined Greek black olives can be kept for 3 to 4 months.

If you notice white scum on the olives or the brine, rinse before using. The scum is just crystallized salt and not bad.

ESCARGOTS IN MUSHROOMS

0.08	$$	275 cals

Serves 4

12 large mushrooms

12 large canned snails

1/2 cup butter or margarine

1 Tbsp vermouth or dry white wine

1 green onion, including top, chopped

2 cloves garlic, minced

1/2 tsp salt

1/4 tsp black pepper

1/4 tsp ground nutmeg

2 Tbsp fresh bread crumbs

1 Wipe mushrooms gently with a barely wet paper towel. Remove stems and refrigerate for other uses. Arrange mushroom caps in a circle on a glass pie plate. Rinse snails in cool water and dry with paper towels. Place 1 snail in each mushroom cap.

2 Place butter in a small microwave-safe bowl. **MW on 30% (medium-low)** for 1 minute, or until soft but not melted. Stir in vermouth, onion, garlic, salt, pepper, and nutmeg. Place a mound of butter mixture on top of each snail. Sprinkle with bread crumbs.

3 Cover assembled mushrooms tightly with heavy plastic wrap. Turning plate halfway around after 1 1/2 minutes, **MW on high** for 3 minutes. Let stand 1 minute before uncovering and serving.

LEFTOVER MUSHROOM STEMS

Don't throw away the stems left over from making stuffed mushrooms. Wipe them with a damp paper towel and trim away any blemishes. Slice stems crosswise and put them into a 2-cup glass measure. If desired, add a teaspoon of butter for flavor. Cover the measure with plastic wrap and **MW on high** for 1 to 1 1/2 minutes per cup. Mushrooms give up their moisture and shrink fast if overcooked; watch them carefully.

When cooked mushroom stems have cooled, put them (including their cooking liquid) into a jar or plastic bag. They will keep in the refrigerator for 4 to 5 days, or they can be frozen for up to a year. Use cooked mushroom stems in any recipe requiring cooked sliced mushrooms.

PORTABLE FOOD TURNTABLES

Sales of microwave cookware reached $400 million in 1984. Of the more than 25 million pieces of cookware sold, the number-one selling item was the portable food rotator manufactured by Nordic Ware and called the Micro-Go-Round. A similar turntable is made by Anchor Hocking.

Some microwave ovens, such as Panasonic and Sharp, have rotating platforms built into them. Portable food rotators are for use in ovens with stationary floors. They can be used to rotate dishes of food weighing 10 lb or less.

Because microwaves cook relatively unevenly, recipes almost always include directions for rotating the dish midway through the cooking. This rotating helps the foods cook evenly throughout; however, turning the dishes is only one way of rotating. Even if you have a turntable in your oven, you must still stir the food or turn some food items upside down during cooking.

Do you need a food rotator? Foods will cook in a microwave oven without one, but if your microwave oven cooks so unevenly that you must turn foods several times to get them done properly, a food rotator might be your answer.

CHEATER'S CHILE RELLENOS

| 0.14 | ✳ | 183 cals |

Serves 8

2 cans (4 oz) whole green chiles

2 cups shredded Longhorn or mild Cheddar cheese, about 8 oz

4 Tbsp all-purpose flour

½ tsp salt

1 cup milk

3 large eggs

chili powder

1 Drain liquid from cans of chiles. Make a lengthwise cut in each chile. Open and lay flat. Remove seeds, which are the fiery part of chiles. Arrange 3 chiles flat on the bottom of a 9-in glass pie plate. Sprinkle with half the cheese. Arrange remaining 3 chiles on top of cheese.

2 Place flour and salt in a mixing bowl. Using a whisk, add milk to flour gradually so that it will not lump. Add eggs and beat well.

3 Pour milk mixture over top of chiles and sprinkle with remaining cheese. Shake a little chile powder on top to make dish attractive.

4 Rotating plate a quarter turn after each 3 minutes of cooking, **MW on 70% (medium high)** for 11 to 13 minutes, or until egg mixture jiggles only slightly. Let stand 15 minutes before serving.

The Brimming Bowlful

In most countries of the world, soup is not an appetizer alone, but a meal. The hearty homemade soups in this section need just bread or crackers, and perhaps a salad course, to satisfy any hungry man. But you can also freeze or refrigerate these soups for hearty bowlfuls later on. If your office has a microwave, take a bowl or mug of soup to work for a robust hot lunch. Leftover soups actually continue to improve in taste as their flavors blend.

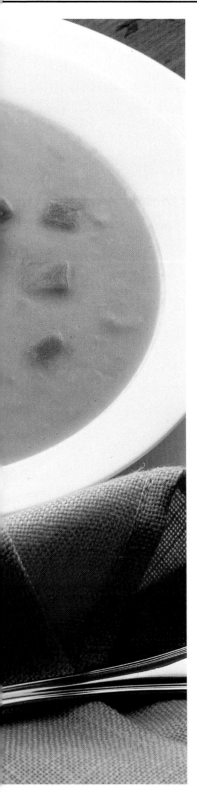

Paul McCartney's Pease Porridge Hot

| *1.30* | ✳ | 253 cals |

Serves 4

1 lb dried peas

2 qt water

2 medium carrots, peeled and chopped

1 large onion, chopped

½ cup finely chopped celery

1 ham bone (optional)

1 cup cooked ham, cubed

2 cups croutons

This is our microwave adaptation of Paul's favorite recipe, Green Pea Soup.

1 Wash and pick out any undesirable peas. Dried peas must be soaked before cooking. There are 2 methods of doing this: (1) overnight soak—add 2 qt cold water, cover, and let stand overnight; or (2) microwave speed soak—add 2 qt hottest tap water. Place peas in a microwave-safe 4-qt pot. Cover with lid and **MW on high** for 10 minutes, or until water boils. Leave covered for 1 hour.

2 Add carrots, onion, celery, ham bone, and cooked ham. Cover and **MW on high** for 30 minutes. Stir and re-cover. **MW on 50% (medium)** for 45 minutes.

3 Remove bone from soup and cut any ham left on it into small chunks. Return meat to soup and discard bone. Add additional ham and stir. (Refrigerate if not serving immediately.) Scatter croutons on top and serve hot.

HEARTY HOMEMADE SOUPS

The best utensil for microwaving soup is either a 2-qt glass batter bowl or a 4-qt microwave-safe simmer pot.

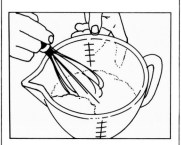

Since soups microwave from all sides (instead of from the bottom only, as in stovetop cooking), it is rarely necessary to stir except to redistribute ingredients midway through cooking to promote even heating.

If you are thickening a soup base with flour, however, you will need to use a wire whisk to blend the ingredients once or twice.

If you do not need the soup immediately, flavors will have more time to blend and develop if you make the soup the day before. When soup has been refrigerated, it is also very easy to skim any fat which rises to the surface.

When reheating soup, stir it first. (Liquids which have been standing for a time may erupt due to a lack of air within.) Outer edges of the soup will reheat more quickly than the center, so you should also stir once or twice during reheating.

Cover soup to speed reheating. A cup of broth will reheat in about 2 minutes on high. For the same amount of a cream-based soup, reheat on 70% (medium-high) for 2 ½ minutes.

RONALD REAGAN'S ONION WINE SOUP

| 0.45 | 🍶 ✳ | 234 cals |

Serves 6

4 Tbsp butter or margarine

5 large onions, chopped

1 large potato, peeled and sliced

¹/₂ cup celery leaves

4 cans (10³/₄-oz) condensed beef broth

1 cup dry white wine

1 Tbsp vinegar

2 tsp sugar

¹/₂ cup milk and ¹/₂ cup heavy cream, or 1 cup half and half

1 Tbsp minced fresh parsley

salt and black pepper to taste

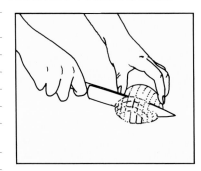

1 Place butter, onions, potato, celery leaves, and 1 can of beef broth into a 4-qt pot. Cover with lid or plastic wrap and **MW on high** for 10 minutes. Stir, re-cover, and MW on high for 10 minutes, or until onions and potato are tender.

2 Place 2 cups of mixture at a time in blender, and puree until smooth. Return mixture to same pot. Add remaining 3 cans of beef broth, white wine, vinegar, and sugar. Re-cover and **MW on high** for 10 minutes, or until mixture begins to boil.

3 Add milk and cream, minced parsley, and salt and pepper to taste. To reheat, set temperature probe to 160°F. on 70% (medium high). Do not allow to boil, as cream will curdle.

PREPARING ONIONS

Onions can be stored in the refrigerator for several months. And when you chop the cool onions, there will be fewer irritating fumes.

To chop onions by hand, use a wooden cutting board and a chef's knife. Cut the onion in half through its axis. Put the onion cut side down on the cutting board. Slice off the top of the onion, and pull the papery skin down over the root end of the onion half. (Do not cut the skin and root off because they will hold the layers of onion together as you slice.) Slice, chop, or mince the onion as desired, or cut it into chunks for chopping in a food processor.

To slice an onion half, hold it with one hand at the root end. Slice crosswise according to the thickness specified in your recipe.

To chop an onion half, hold it as you would for slicing. Make lengthwise slices through the onion at ¹/₄-in intervals ending at the root, then make ¹/₄-in crosswise slices. These slices will release the onion pieces.

To mince, chop the onion first, then put the palm of one hand on top of the blunt side of the knife near the point. Holding the point of the knife on the cutting board, rock the knife blade up and down onto the chopped onion until it is chopped very fine.

If you have a food processor, use the steel blade to chop an onion. Put chunks of onion into the processor bowl and pulse the motor on and off until the onion is chopped.

Chicken Tortilla Soup

| 0.20 | ✳ * | 71 cals |

*freeze without chips

Serves 6

½ cup chopped onion

1 can (16-oz) tomatoes, drained with liquid reserved

4 cups chicken broth, homemade or canned

1 can (4-oz) chopped green chiles, with liquid

1 cup shredded cooked chicken

1 Tbsp fresh lime juice

salt and black pepper to taste

regular-size corn chips

thin slices of fresh lime

1 Place onion in a 2-qt glass batter bowl. Cover with plastic wrap and **MW on high** for 3 minutes.

2 Add liquid from canned tomatoes to bowl. Mash tomatoes or chop in food processor, and add to onion mixture.

3 Add broth, chiles, including liquid, shredded chicken, lime juice, salt, and pepper. Re-cover and **MW on high** for 16 minutes, or set temperature probe for 170°F.

4 Add ¼ cup corn chips to each soup portion, and float a slice of lime in the center.

ITALIAN VEGETABLE SOUP

| 0.30 | ✳ | 186 cals |

Serves 8

12 oz fully cooked link sausage

1 medium onion, chopped

1 can (16-oz) tomato sauce

1 can (15-oz) garbanzo beans, with liquid

1 can (10½-oz) condensed beef broth

1½ cups water

½ lb zucchini, sliced ¼ in thick

1 bay leaf

1 tsp dried basil leaves

¼ tsp garlic powder

¼ tsp freshly ground black pepper

grated Parmesan cheese

1 Cut sausage into ¼-in-thick slices and combine with onion in a 4-qt pot. Cover with lid or plastic wrap and **MW on high** for 5 to 6 minutes; drain.

2 Into same pot, add tomato sauce, beans including liquid, beef broth, water, zucchini, bay leaf, basil, garlic powder, and pepper; stir. Re-cover and **MW on high** for 20 minutes. Let soup stand until zucchini is desired doneness. To serve, sprinkle individual portions with cheese.

PARMESAN CHEESE

If you have a food processor, it is very easy to grate hard cheeses such as Parmesan. Bring cheese to room temperature, then cut into 1-in chunks. Using the steel chopping blade, lock the lid and turn motor on. Drop chunks of cheese through feed tube and run processor for 1 or 2 minutes, or until cheese resembles tapioca.

CORN AND OYSTER BISQUE

0.20	286 cals

Serves 6

1 jar (12-oz) fresh shucked oysters

4 Tbsp margarine or butter

1/2 cup finely chopped onion

4 Tbsp finely chopped celery

4 Tbsp all-purpose flour

1 can (10-oz) condensed chicken broth

1 cup milk

2 tsp Worcestershire sauce

1/2 tsp celery salt

2 cans (16-oz each) cream-style corn

1 In shellfish cookery, the "liquor" is the liquid from oysters, scallops, and so on. Drain liquor from oysters and set aside. Rinse oysters and chop coarsely; set aside.

2 Place margarine, onion, and celery in a 2-qt batter bowl. Cover with plastic wrap and **MW on high** for 4 to 5 minutes.

3 Using a whisk, blend in flour. Whisk in broth, milk, Worcestershire sauce, celery salt, and reserved oyster liquor. Whisking every 3 minutes, **MW on high** for 7 to 8 minutes, or until thickened.

4 Whisk in corn and oysters. Just before serving, **MW on high** to desired temperature, or 160°F. if using temperature probe.

5 This soup is traditionally topped with a dollop of unsweetened whipped cream, and served with strips of toasted bread called "sippets."

OYSTERS

According to superstition, oysters should not be eaten in months lacking the letter *r* in their name (May through August). That's because before refrigeration, oysters would spoil rapidly during these warm months. The superstition has been disproved; now oysters can be eaten all year long, although they are at peak quality in winter and early spring.

When purchasing live oysters, make certain the shells are tightly closed. Closed shells mean the oysters are alive. Refrigerate oysters and make sure they can breathe (store in basket or open paper bag, for example). Use them within a week.

Shucked oysters (out of shell) are packed by the pint, quart, or gallon. Depending on size, a pint of shucked oysters may contain between 20 and 50 oysters. The oysters should be plump and cream colored, and the liquor should be clear. Refrigerate shucked oysters and use them within 2 days of purchase.

LYNDON JOHNSON'S PEDERNALES RIVER CHILI

| 0.23 | ✳ | 441 cals |

Serves 6

2 lb coarsely ground beef

1 medium onion, chopped

3 to 6 tsp chili powder

1 clove garlic, minced, about 1 tsp

1 tsp dried oregano

1 tsp cumin seed

1 can (16-oz) sliced stewed tomatoes, with liquid

1 can (12-oz) beer

2 dashes Tabasco sauce

salt to taste

1 can (16-oz) kidney beans, drained (optional)

1 Crumble beef into a dishwasher-safe plastic colander. Sprinkle onion on top. Set colander in a 4-qt pot. **MW on high** for 4 minutes.

2 Stir to break up cooked beef and redistribute uncooked areas **MW on high** for 4 minutes, or until beef is no longer pink.

3 Pour grease into a can; refrigerate and discard when it solidifies. Transfer beef to same pot.

4 Stir chili powder, garlic, oregano, and cumin seed into beef. Add canned tomatoes including liquid. Pour 3/4 cup of beer into the pot and drink the rest! Add Tabasco sauce and salt to taste; stir. Do not cover pot. **MW on high** for 12 minutes.

5 President Johnson did not put beans in his chili. If you like them in yours, add and **MW on high** until heated through.

CHILI COOKOFFS

The first chili cookoff in Texas was held in 1967, in Terlingua, a dusty ghost town near Big Bend National Park. This annual event now attracts more than 30,000 spectators. The people we've met at chili cookoffs have all been fun-loving, generous, patriotic, free-spirited Americans. Chili cooks (known as "chiliheads") are also free with their spirits. It's often seemed that chili cookoffs were just an excuse to drink beer, one of the standard ingredients in Texas chili.

There are as many ways of fixing chili as there are chili cooks. However, there are 3 main ingredients always found in Texas chili: meat (usually beef), chili powder, and beer. If there are beans in your chili, it's definitely NOT Texas chili!

Authentic Texas chili is not made with ground beef. Discriminating chili cooks hand-cut a beef roast into small chunks of meat, each the size of a sugar cube. Texas supermarkets usually have a coarse ground beef available, labelled chili grind. However, chili made with regular ground beef cooks faster and is always tender.

The beer in chili serves as a meat tenderizer, and cooked chili does not taste at all like beer. If you want, substitute water in an equal amount, but it won't taste quite as robust!

Meat from the Deep

Fish and shellfish are some of the most successful foods to microwave. They cook fast and are very tender. But they can also overcook easily and become tough if microwaved too long. When microwaving seafood, place it in the oven just before serving to avoid having to reheat it. You can use your microwave to help defrost seafood, too, but be careful not to thaw it in the microwave too long, lest the edges begin to cook. For best results, finish the defrosting at room temperature.

AN HONEST SOLE

| 0.08 | $ | 200 cals |

Serves 2

¹/₃ cup sliced almonds

1 tsp margarine or butter

8 oz fresh sole fillets (see note)

1 Tbsp lemon juice

chopped fresh parsley

salt and black pepper to taste

paprika

lemon wedges

1 Place almonds and margarine in a 1-cup glass measure. **MW on high** for 1 minute.

2 Stir well to distribute margarine. Stirring every minute, **MW on high** for 2 to 3 minutes, or until the almonds are toasted. Set aside.

3 Put fish fillets into a glass pie plate. Sprinkle with lemon juice and parsley. Cover with waxed paper. **MW on high** for 3 minutes, or until fish flakes easily.

4 If desired, add salt, pepper, and paprika. Transfer fillets to dinner plates and top with toasted almonds. Place a lemon wedge on each plate.

NOTE
Frozen sole fillets may also be used. Use microwave timing suggested on package, or add 1 to 2 minutes to above time.

Serving Suggestion
To complete the dinner, add a potato casserole or baked potatoes. This delectable European fish is usually served with a white Burgundy wine. For dessert, make Homemade Brownies (page 157) and serve with fresh fruit.

DEFROSTING FISH

One way to defrost frozen fish is to transfer it from the freezer to the refrigerator a few hours before you need it. Put the package into a dish because, as it thaws, fish will leak.

You can defrost fish in the microwave oven, but watch it carefully because it can "cook" around the edges while the center stays frozen. If you are defrosting a 1-lb rectangular box, cover both long ends with aluminum foil to reflect microwaves off these areas, which tend to thaw the fastest. **MW on 30% (medium-low)** for 4 minutes, then turn the box upside down and **MW** for 4 minutes more.

Be especially careful when defrosting shrimp or other shellfish in the microwave. Since they are small, individual pieces that are irregularly shaped, the shellfish can easily be microwaved too long and begin to cook. Separate the pieces as soon as they start to thaw, and remove from oven. Run cool water over them to finish defrosting, then continue with recipe.

HEALTHY HALIBUT

0.18	188 cals

Serves 2

1 1/2 **cups sliced fresh mushrooms**

2/3 **cup thinly sliced onions**

1/3 **cup chopped tomato**

4 **Tbsp chopped green bell pepper**

4 **Tbsp chopped fresh parsley**

3 **Tbsp chopped pimiento**

2 **halibut steaks or 4 flounder fillets, about 1 lb total**

salt and black pepper

1/4 **tsp dillweed**

4 **Tbsp dry white wine**

2 **Tbsp fresh lemon juice**

lemon wedges

1 Place mushrooms, onions, tomato, and bell pepper in a 4-cup glass measure. Cover with plastic wrap and **MW on high** for 3 to 4 minutes. Add parsley and pimiento. Set aside.

2 Arrange fish in an 8-in round glass dish with thick areas of fish toward the outside of the dish. Sprinkle with salt, pepper, and dillweed. Drain liquid from cooked vegetable mixture; discard. Distribute vegetables over top of fish. Pour wine and lemon juice evenly over all.

3 Cover dish with waxed paper. Turning dish halfway around after 2 minutes, **MW on high** for 4 to 5 minutes, or until fish flakes apart with a fork. Serve with lemon wedges.

Serving Suggestion
Since this fish is topped with an assortment of chopped vegetables, accompany it with a simple starch vegetable, such as Double-Cheese Stuffed Potatoes (page 153), and perhaps a romaine lettuce salad. Serve with a white Portuguese wine.

NOTE
Halibut is the largest member of the flounder family. A 100-g raw weight portion of halibut has 21 g of protein, less than 1 g of fat, and only 97 calories. We've adapted this recipe from one by the American Heart Association. It is low in calories as well as low in cholesterol.

FISH SUBSTITUTIONS
If you want to make a recipe but don't have the fish specified, other varieties can be substituted. According to the U.S. Department of Commerce and the National Marine Fisheries Service, the following are groups of fish varieties that are similar in flavor and type.

White meat, very light, delicate flavor
Cod
Cusk
Dover Sole
Haddock
Lake Whitefish
Pacific Halibut
Pacific Sanddab
Petrale Sole
Rex Sole
Southern Flounder
Spotted Cabrilla
Summer Flounder (Fluke)
Witch Flounder
Yellowtail Flounder
Yellowtail Snapper

White meat, light to moderate flavor
American Plaice/Dab
Arrowtooth Flounder
Butterfish
Catfish
Cobia
English Sole
Lingcod
Mahi Mahi
Pacific Whiting
Red Snapper
Rock Sole
Sauger
Snook
Spotted Sea Trout
Starry Flounder
White King Salmon
White Sea Trout
Whiting
Winter Flounder
Wolffish

Light meat, very light, delicate flavor
Alaska Pollock
Brook Trout
Giant Sea Bass
Grouper
Pacific Ocean Perch
Rainbow Trout
Smelt
Tautog
Walleye
White Crappie
White Sea Bass

Light meat, light to moderate flavor
Atlantic Ocean Perch
Atlantic Salmon
Black Drum
Buffalofish
Burbot
Carp
Chum Salmon
Crevalle Jack
Croaker
Eel
Greenland Turbot
Jewfish
King (Chinook) Salmon
Lake Chub
Lake Herring
Lake Sturgeon
Lake Trout
Monkfish
Mullet
Northern Pike
Perch
Pink Salmon
Pollock
Pompano
Rockfish
Sablefish
Sand Shark
Sculpin
Scup/Porgie
Sheepshead
Silver (Coho) Salmon
Spot
Striped Bass
Swordfish
Vermilion Snapper

Light meat, more pronounced flavor
Atlantic Mackerel
King Mackerel
Spanish Mackerel

Darker meat, light to moderate flavor
Black Seabass
Bluefish
Ocean Pout
Sockeye (Red) Salmon

FLOUNDERING AROUND

0.07	344 cals

Serves 2

1 lb flounder fillets, thawed

1/3 cup grated Parmesan cheese

2 green onions including tops, sliced

2 Tbsp mayonnaise

4 tsp fresh lemon juice

1/4 tsp salt

dash of Tabasco

paprika

1 Place flounder fillets in an 8-in round glass dish. Arrange fillets in a circle so that the thin ends of each fillet are overlapping each other.

2 In a small bowl, combine cheese, green onions, mayonnaise, lemon juice, salt, and Tabasco. Stir to mix well.

3 Spread mixture over fish. Sprinkle with paprika. Turning dish halfway around after 2 minutes, **MW on high** for 4 to 5 minutes, or until fish is opaque. Transfer to individual plates and serve.

Serving Suggestion

A simple green vegetable, such as Mushroom Broccoli Spears (page 151) makes a pleasant accompaniment to this entree, which has a rich topping. Serve with a dry white wine. If no starchy food is served with dinner, Old-Fashioned Rice Custard (page 157) makes a pleasing dessert.

SALMON STEAKS WITH CUCUMBER SAUCE

| 0.15 | $$ | 561 cals |

Serves 2

¹/₂ cup grated peeled cucumber

salt and freshly ground pepper

1 carton (6-oz) plain yogurt

1 Tbsp chopped fresh parsley

¹/₂ cup dry white wine

1 Tbsp fresh lemon juice

2 fresh salmon steaks, about 1 lb total

1 Sprinkle cucumber with salt and pepper. Let stand in bowl 10 to 15 minutes. Press cucumber to drain liquid. Add yogurt and parsley to drained cucumber. Set aside.

2 Put wine and lemon juice into a 1-qt casserole dish. Cover with lid or plastic wrap. **MW on high** for 2 minutes or until boiling.

3 Carefully place fish in wine. Re-cover and **MW on high**

for 2¹/₂ to 3 minutes. Let stand, covered, 3 minutes. Using a slotted spoon, remove fish from wine. Serve with sauce.

Serving Suggestion

Since salmon is a specialty of the Pacific Northwest, vegetables of American origin make a nice addition to this dinner. Try zucchini or corn, and serve with sourdough bread. Serve with a chilled rosé wine.

INEFFABLE CRAB NEWBURG

| 0.15 | 🍴 | $ $ | 275 cals |

Serves 4

2 cups lump crab meat

2 Tbsp margarine or butter

2 Tbsp all-purpose flour

2 cups milk

3 large eggs, well beaten

pinch of dry mustard

3 Tbsp dry sherry

salt and black pepper to taste

paprika

chopped fresh parsley for garnish

An editorial in the *Baltimore Sun*, a newspaper which should have the last word in crab information, has written about the *ineffable* crab. The word means, "too overwhelming to be described in words."

1 Pick over crab meat carefully, and remove small bits of shell or cartilage. Set aside.

2 Put margarine in a 2-qt batter bowl. **MW on high** for 30 seconds, or until melted.

3 Using a wire whisk, blend in flour. Gradually stir in milk. Whisking midway through cooking, **MW on high** for 5 to 6 minutes, or until mixture begins to bubble.

4 Whisk in eggs, mustard, and sherry. Add crab meat. **MW on 70% (medium-high)** for 3 minutes, or until mixture is serving temperature. If serving later, reheat mixture carefully, because the eggs will curdle if cooked too long.

Serving Suggestion
This can be served over steamed rice, toast, or pastry shells. Garnish the servings with paprika and parsley. Add a tossed salad containing a variety of fresh raw vegetables. Since the entree is in a rich cream sauce, use a simple oil and vinegar dressing on the salad. Serve with a light white wine.

CRAB MEAT

One of our most flavorful foods in the United States is the blue crab. During the Maryland crab season, which extends from April 1 to January 1, more crabs are harvested from the Chesapeake Bay than anywhere else in the world.

Live crabs can be purchased by the bushel. Picked crab meat is sold in several forms. Lump or backfin meat is large whole lumps from the body of the crab. Special meat includes the normal mixed proportion of lump and loose crab meat found in the body. Regular or flake includes all the meat from the body except lump. Claw meat is only from the appendages.

Fresh picked crab meat should be a white or slightly off-white color. It should have a fresh odor or light ocean scent. Once it starts to deteriorate, crab meat takes on a sour smell and then an ammonia odor. Once the ammonia odor is detected, the crab meat should be discarded.

Senator Lloyd Bentsen's Texas Seafood Dinner

| 0.15 | $ $ | 506 cals |

Serves 4

1 cup chopped celery

¹/₂ cup chopped green bell pepper

4 Tbsp chopped onion

1 cup shelled and deveined shrimp

1 cup flaked crab meat

1 cup mayonnaise

2 Tbsp dry sherry

1 Tbsp fresh lemon juice

1 tsp Worcestershire sauce

¹/₂ tsp Tabasco sauce

salt and black pepper to taste

2 slices whole-wheat bread

1 Put celery, bell pepper, and onion in a 4-cup glass measure. Cover with plastic wrap and **MW on high** for 4 minutes.

2 Add shrimp, re-cover, and **MW on high** for 3 minutes. Drain liquids well and discard.

3 Pick over crab meat carefully, and remove small bits of shell or cartilage. Add crab meat, mayonnaise, sherry, lemon juice, Worcestershire sauce, and Tabasco to cooked vegetables. Add salt and pepper to taste and stir mixture well.

4 Tear bread slices into chunks and put in a blender or food processor. Pulse to make fine crumbs. Sprinkle half the crumbs into the bottom of either 4 scallop shells, 4 individual ramekins, or a 1-qt casserole. Spoon seafood mixture onto crumbs and sprinkle remaining crumbs on top. **MW on 70% (medium-high)** for 5 minutes, or until heated through.

Serving Suggestion

Begin this dinner with a fresh fruit cocktail or simple broth-based soup. Accompany the rich entree with a simple green vegetable, such as Tahitian Green Beans (page 150), and serve it with a white wine from the Texas Hill Country. If dessert is to be served, try a small square of Texas Crude Cake (page 111).

PAINTING WITH FOOD

The dishes a cook delivers to the table should be as pretty as a picture. To have every item of a meal the same color would be unappetizing. But a rosy ham, accompanied by yellow corn and a tossed green salad with blushing tomatoes—there is a picture van Gogh might have painted if he'd had the groceries.

Next, think of flavor. Your goal is a bouquet—no 2 flavors alike, but all pleasantly contrasting. Textures should contrast, too. It is not difficult to achieve; it only means a little planning and a touch of imagination.

CELERY

The supermarket usually displays bunches of celery with leaves attached. When selecting celery, choose a light-green bunch with fresh-looking leaves; bunches with thin, dark-green ribs may be tough and stringy.

Cut the root end off and wash each rib well, then drain excess water. Cut off the leaves and put into a small plastic bag. (If leaves are left on the ribs, they tend to spoil quickly and can make the celery ribs turn soft.) Put cleaned celery in a plastic bag and seal tightly.

Celery leaves can be used in salads or to flavor soups and stews. To make raw celery sticks, place 1 rib on a cutting board. Use a chef's knife to cut the rib into 3 lengthwise strips. Then cut strips crosswise into 3-in sticks. To chop celery, begin cutting a rib the same way, but then chop the lengthwise strips into 1/4-in pieces.

Celery can be sliced 2 different ways. Hold the knife perpendicular to the cutting board to slice whole ribs crosswise. Or slice it diagonally by holding the knife slanted at a 45° angle while slicing whole ribs crosswise. Chopped celery is not interchangeable with sliced celery in a recipe because slices take longer to cook.

SHRIMP ÉTOUFFÉE

| 0.28 | 🍳 | $ $ | 400 cals |

Serves 4

6 Tbsp butter or margarine

1¹/₂ cups chopped onions

¹/₂ cup chopped green bell pepper

¹/₂ cup chopped celery

3 cloves garlic, minced

1 Tbsp cornstarch

1 Tbsp Worcestershire sauce

1 Tbsp paprika

¹/₃ cup water

4 Tbsp chili sauce

1 Tbsp fresh lemon juice

¹/₂ tsp cayenne pepper

1 lb shrimp, peeled and deveined

chopped fresh parsley for garnish

This Cajun dish is usually made with crawfish, but is equally good with shrimp.

1 Combine butter, onions, bell pepper, celery, and garlic in a 2-qt casserole. Cover with lid or plastic wrap and **MW on high** for 10 minutes, stirring once midway through cooking.

2 Stir cornstarch, Worcestershire, and paprika into onion mixture. Blend until no lumps of cornstarch can be seen. Add water, chili sauce, lemon juice, and cayenne pepper; stir. Stir in shrimp and re-cover. **MW on high** for 8 minutes, or until shrimp are pink. Garnish with fresh parsley.

Serving Suggestion
This hearty Creole dish would go well with a Louisiana beer, such as Dixie. Accompany the entree with rice and a Caesar salad. For dessert, have one of George Bush's Pralines (page 128).

PREPARING SHRIMP
To peel and devein shrimp, hold the tail end of one of the shrimp in one hand. Slip the thumb of your other hand under the shell between the feelers, and lift off several segments of shell. Then, holding tail firmly, pull out shrimp from rest of shell and tail.

To devein shrimp, use a small sharp knife.

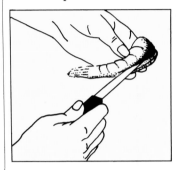

Cut about ¹/₈ in deep along the outside curve of the shrimp and lift out the intestinal tract.

Rinse shrimp in cool water, then lay on a paper towel to drain. Pat shrimp dry before using.

SEAFARERS' SHRIMP & SCALLOPS

| 0.10 | $$ | 392 cals |

Serves 2

½ lb shrimp in the shell

½ lb scallops, rinsed

4 Tbsp butter or margarine

1 medium lime

¼ tsp garlic powder, or 2 cloves fresh garlic, minced

paprika

1 Tbsp chopped fresh parsley

This recipe is from Tony Breard, a USNA classmate of John's from Monroe, Louisiana. Tony says that this recipe "serves 2 landlubbers or 1 seafarer." We must be landlubbers, because there was more than enough for the two of us!

1 Peel and devein shrimp. Place shrimp and scallops into a 1-qt casserole dish.

2 Put butter in a 1-cup glass measure. **MW on high** for 40 seconds, or until melted.

3 Pour melted butter evenly over shellfish. Cut lime in half and squeeze all the juice onto the shellfish. Add garlic and sprinkle with paprika. Top shellfish with parsley.

4 Cover dish with waxed paper. Stirring after every minute, **MW on high** for 3 to 4 minutes, or until shrimp are opaque. (Cooking shellfish too long makes them tough and rubbery.)

Serving Suggestion
Serve over rice or dip French bread into the butter sauce. A large tossed salad is a nice accompaniment, along with a dry white wine, such as a Côtes de Provence.

SCALLOPS

The only part of a scallop that is eaten is the muscle which opens and closes the shell. But the scallop shell itself is a natural dish in which foods can be cooked. In the United States, scallops are sold already shucked, but you can buy shells in specialty shops.

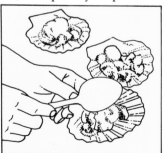

There are 2 varieties of scallops. Tiny bay scallops are available locally according to region and season, but mostly from October to April. They are sweet and delicately flavored. Sea scallops are larger and available year round. They are succulent and tender, but for some recipes, cut them in half.

Scallops are low in fat and calories. Microwave them just until they turn opaque. They can easily overcook and become tough.

Frozen scallops bear no resemblance to fresh, in taste or texture. But they also can be cooked quickly in a microwave.

WINE HANDLING

Before bottles of wine are opened, they should be stored in a dark, fairly cool place away from drafts, air-conditioning vents, or heating elements. Store bottles on their sides so that their corks stay moist. If corks dry out, they shrink and let in air, which spoils the wine. A dry cork is difficult to remove from a bottle because it crumbles.

Almost all red wines should be served at cool room temperature. White wines, roses, and champagnes should be lightly chilled. Do not let them get too cold. Place the bottle in the refrigerator for two or three hours, or chill it in an ice bucket for 15 to 20 minutes before serving.

Once a wine has been opened, it cannot be recorked and returned to storage. Left-over dinner wines should be refrigerated, but drink them within a week or two, or use them in cooking. Opened bottles of fortified wines (such as Sherry, Port, Madeira, and Marsala) should be kept on a cool, dark shelf. Cap or close them with a bottle stopper.

In cooking, wines are used primarily for flavor, since the alcoholic content evaporates as it cooks. The acidity of wine helps tenderize meats, both during marinating and cooking. Never use cooking wines, which are found in supermarkets in the vinegar section. They have added salt and are inferior in quality. One philosophy is that you should never cook with a wine you wouldn't drink.

PAELLA CASABLANCA

1.00 ❑ ✳ * 495 cals
*freeze without clams

Serves 4

1 clove garlic, peeled

1 large onion

1 green bell pepper

2 Tbsp olive oil

2 cans (10¾-oz) condensed chicken broth

1 cup chopped cooked chicken or turkey

½ cup chopped cooked ham

1 cup raw rice

⅛ tsp saffron, or 1 tsp ground turmeric

crushed red pepper or cayenne to taste

½ lb shrimp, peeled and deveined

1 cup frozen peas

1 jar (2-oz) sliced pimientoes

8 hard-shelled clams in the shell (cherrystone or littleneck)

1 Chop vegetables by hand or use a food processor. If using a processor, insert steel blade, turn motor on, and drop garlic into feed tube; garlic is minced when no chunks are visible. Remove skin from onion and cut onion into large chunks. Remove stem and seeds from bell pepper, and cut into chunks. Put onion and bell pepper into food processor bowl. Pulse motor on and off briefly until vegetables are chopped to the size of peas.

2 Put garlic, onion, bell pepper, and olive oil into a 4-qt pot. Cover with lid or plastic wrap and **MW on high** for 4 minutes.

3 Add broth, chicken and ham. Re-cover and **MW on high** for 10 minutes.

4 Stir in rice and saffron or turmeric. Re-cover and **MW on high** for 18 to 20 minutes, or until rice has absorbed liquid and is tender. Stir in shrimp, peas, and pimiento.

5 Scrub clams and arrange in a circle on top of mixture, with hinge of shell toward the center and outside of shells to the edge of pot. Re-cover and **MW on high** for 8 to 10 minutes, or until clam shells have opened. Rotate pot a half turn midway in cooking.

6 Discard any clams that do not open, then serve at once.

Serving Suggestion
This substantial main dish needs only bread, or perhaps a simple mixed lettuce salad with a vinaigrette dressing. Serve with a chilled Portuguese rosé wine.

GOOD TASTING TABLECLOTHS
You can fall in love with a dinner at first sight, or you can be glad it's only a one-night stand. Appearance is very important. An average meal can look good, and a good meal can seem outstanding if served in an effective setting. Maybe that's why we have such an aversion to food served in an aluminum foil tray!

The table setting doesn't have to include silver and bone china on a white linen tablecloth. There's nothing as appealing (or as inexpensive) as a candle casting a flattering light from the neck of an empty rafia-covered wine bottle that's sitting on a checkered tablecloth.

Meat on the Wing

One of the most healthful meats you can eat is also one of the best to microwave. Chicken remains tender while cooking fast on high power. Since poultry parts have irregular shapes, always arrange them for even microwaving with the thick areas toward the outside of the dish and the bony areas in the center. Whether it is a recipe from the Orient, Pakistan, the Middle East, Europe, or the Americas, the poultry will be delicious when microwaved.

Senator John Warner's Virginia Stuffed Chicken

| 0.35 | ✳ | 765 cals |

Serves 4

2 Tbsp margarine or butter

1 rib celery, chopped

1 small onion, chopped

½ cup milk

1 large egg, lightly beaten

½ tsp onion salt

½ tsp dried basil

¼ tsp black pepper

2 cups dry stuffing mix

1 roasting chicken, about 3 lb

Kitchen Bouquet or Micro Shake

1 Put margarine, celery, and onion in a 4-cup glass measure. Cover with plastic wrap and **MW on high** for 3 minutes.

2 Stir in milk, egg, onion salt, basil, and pepper. Add stuffing mix and stir to moisten evenly. Set aside.

3 Remove giblets and neck from inside chicken. Set giblets aside for gravy. Rinse chicken in cool water, inside and out. Pat dry, using paper towels. Spoon prepared stuffing into chicken cavity. Use trussing string or dental floss to tie legs together. Rub chicken with Kitchen Bouquet or sprinkle with Micro Shake so it will appear brown and appealing.

4 Using small pieces of aluminum foil, cover drumstick ends and wings to prevent them from overcooking. Place chicken breast side down in a 2-qt rectangular glass dish. **MW on 70% (medium-high)** for 15 minutes.

5 Turn chicken breast side up and **MW on 70%** for 15 minutes. Let stand 10 minutes before cutting into chicken to test for doneness. Carve and serve with giblet gravy.

Serving Suggestion

Asparagus with French Mustard Sauce (page 149) goes well with this stuffed poultry. Serve with a light Virginia wine. For dessert, try Ronald Reagan's Pumpkin Pecan Pie (page 156).

Giblet Gravy

Makes 1 to 2 cups

giblets from chicken

all-purpose flour

Kitchen Bouquet

salt and black pepper to taste

1 While chicken is in microwave oven, make gravy on conventional range. Rinse giblets in cool water; drain. Place giblets in small saucepan. Add hottest tap water just to cover giblets. Bring water just to boiling, then turn down heat until liquid barely simmers. Cover and simmer 20 minutes.

2 When giblets are tender, remove to a plate and let cool. Skim fat from top of liquid (see page 68). Measure liquid and set aside 1 Tbsp flour per cup of liquid. Do not stir flour directly into the hot liquid, because it will lump; combine flour with the same amount of cool water in a small bowl; blend with whisk.

3 Blend flour mixture into hot liquid. Add Kitchen Bouquet a few drops at a time until gravy is the color you like. Add salt and pepper to taste. Return saucepan to heat and cook just until mixture begins to boil so that gravy will thicken. Cut cooked giblets into small pieces and add them to gravy. Discard chicken neck.

CHICKEN AND CELERY SEED DUMPLINGS

| 0.55 🍴 ✳ | 712 cals |

Serves 4

| 1 3-lb chicken, cut into parts |
| 1 large onion, cut into chunks |
| 4 medium carrots, peeled and sliced into rounds |
| 2 ribs celery, sliced diagonally |
| 3 cups hottest tap water |
| 3 tsp instant chicken bouillon granules |
| 1 bay leaf |
| ¼ tsp black pepper |
| ⅛ tsp poultry seasoning |
| 3 Tbsp cornstarch |
| ⅓ cup cool water |
| 1 cup Bisquick or other biscuit mix |
| ⅓ cup milk |
| ½ tsp celery seeds |

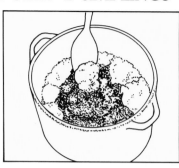

1 Remove package of giblets from chicken and freeze to use for another purpose. Rinse chicken in cool water. Arrange chicken parts in a 4-qt pot so that the thick pieces are toward the outside of the pot and the bony parts are in the center.

2 Add onion, carrots, celery, water, bouillon, bay leaf, pepper, and poultry seasoning. Cover with lid or plastic wrap. **MW on high** for 20 minutes.

3 Turn each piece of chicken over and stir other ingredients in pot to redistribute them. Re-cover and **MW on high** for 10 to 15 minutes, or until vegetables are tender.

4 Remove chicken from pot and set aside on a plate. In a small bowl, mix cornstarch with ⅓ cup cool water. Blend well into liquid in pot. Stirring after half of cooking, **MW on high** for 4 to 5 minutes, or until thickened. Return chicken to pot.

5 To make dumplings, mix Bisquick, milk and celery seeds in a bowl. Drop batter 1 Tbsp at a time around the outer sides of the pot. Cover. **MW on high** for 5 to 6 minutes, turning pot a half turn after 3 minutes.

Serving Suggestion
Accompany with a congealed salad, such as aspic. This homey American dish really doesn't need wine.

MICROWAVING CHICKEN

Chicken microwaves most evenly if cut into uniformly sized parts. Separate the drumstick from the thigh, and split the whole breast in half. Make a triangle shape with the wing, tucking the tip behind its first joint.

Arrange assorted chicken pieces so that the meaty portions are toward the sides of the dish and the thin or bony pieces (such as wings and drumstick ends) are in the center. Turn each piece over and rearrange after half cooking. Cover the chicken to retain the heat and prevent splatters.

Chicken will continue to cook after microwaving. Allow to stand about ⅓ of the microwaving time before checking for doneness. You can always add more cooking time if necessary.

CUTTING UP A CHICKEN

Whole chickens are usually cheaper at the supermarket than those already cut up. To cut one up yourself, first remove the neck and giblets. (They can be used to make Giblet Gravy, see page 47.) Place the chicken on a cutting board breast side up.

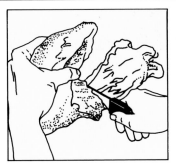

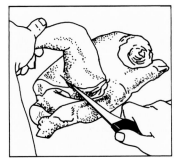

Cut through ribs at each side of chicken to separate back from breast. Divide breast into 2 halves by bending it backward until the breastbone snaps. Cut along the breastbone, leaving it attached to one breast half. Instead of a whole chicken, you should now have 8 chicken parts plus the backbone.

Pull one leg (thigh and drumstick connected) away from body and cut through the skin between leg and breast. Lift the chicken and bend leg until hip joint cracks. Cut through joint and remove leg. Repeat with the other leg. Cut drumsticks and thighs apart to make 4 pieces.

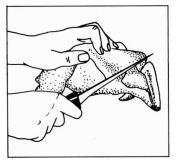

Remove the wings in the same manner. Fold the wings into triangular shapes by tucking wing tip behind first joint.

Moorghi Shahi

| 0.30 | ✳ | 644 cals |

Serves 4

3 lb chicken pieces

1 Tbsp instant minced onion

¼ tsp instant minced garlic

1 Tbsp water

1 Tbsp fresh lemon juice

1 tsp salt

½ tsp ground turmeric

¼ tsp coarsely ground black pepper

1 can (19-oz) chick peas or ceci, drained

1 medium tomato, chopped

1 Tbsp cornstarch

1 Tbsp sesame seeds

paprika

In Urdu, an Indian language, the name of this recipe means "the King's Chicken."

1 Place chicken skin side down in a 2-qt rectangular glass dish. Arrange pieces so that the meaty portions are toward the outside of the dish, and the bony pieces or ends are in the center. Cover with waxed paper. **MW on high** for 8 minutes.

2 Turn each piece over and arrange as before. Re-cover and **MW on high** for 8 minutes.

3 Meanwhile, combine onion, garlic, water, lemon juice, salt, turmeric, and pepper in a mixing bowl. Let stand until onion and garlic absorb liquid and become soft. Add chick peas and tomato. Stir in cornstarch.

4 After chicken has been microwaved, drain liquid from chicken into tomato mixture; stir. Pour mixture over pieces and sprinkle with sesame seeds and paprika. Re-cover and **MW on high** for 6 to 8 minutes.

5 Let stand for 5 minutes. Test to see if chicken is done and add extra microwaving time if necessary.

Serving Suggestion
Since this entree already contains several vegetables, add some simple but elegant fresh artichokes to complete the dinner (see page 149). Open some Greek white wine with the meal, and serve Bill Steiner's Luscious Lemon Cake (page 112) for dessert.

DEFROSTING CHICKEN

To defrost chicken parts in the microwave, remove packaging and place in the dish required for the recipe. (Defrosting will be more rapid without the insulation of plastic wrap and foam meat trays.) **MW on 30% (medium-low)** for 5 to 7 minutes per pound.

After half the defrosting time, turn the chicken upside down. Separate the parts as soon as possible. If some areas of the chicken have thawed while others are still frozen, use small pieces of aluminum foil to cover the thawed areas.

Remove thin or bony pieces (such as wings or drumsticks) from the oven as soon as they thaw. Leave breasts and thighs in the oven for the remaining time, because they take longer to defrost. Rinse in cool water and pat dry with paper towels before cooking.

Chicken Italiano

| 0.20 | ✳ | 514 cals |

Serves 2

1 lb chicken parts (breasts, drumsticks, or thighs)

1 can (16-oz) stewed tomatoes, with liquid

½ can (6-oz) tomato paste

1 tsp dried basil

¼ tsp garlic powder

1 medium zucchini squash, sliced ¼ in thick

cooked noodles or pasta (see page 146)

grated Parmesan cheese

1 Rinse chicken in cool water and pat dry using paper towels. Place in a round 2-qt casserole. Arrange chicken skin side down, with the meaty portions toward the outside. Cover with casserole lid or plastic wrap and **MW on high** for 4 minutes.

2 Turn each piece of chicken skin side up and arrange as before. In a small mixing bowl, combine stewed tomatoes (including liquid), tomato paste, basil, and garlic powder. Pour over chicken. Re-cover and **MW on high** for 6 to 7 minutes.

3 Add zucchini to casserole; re-cover. **MW on high** for 3 minutes. Serve over cooked noodles and sprinkle with cheese.

Serving Suggestion

Serve Joe Paterno's Antipasto (page 12) as a first course before this Italian entree, which is served over cooked noodles and topped with grated Parmesan cheese. Add garlic bread for hearty eaters. What else to drink with this meal but a Chianti Classico!

FROZEN CHICKEN PRODUCTS

Drums and dipsters, pieces and patties, chunks, nuggets, and rondelets! They're all forms of chicken frozen in a box. According to their packages, these frozen chicken products can be "crispy, original, fried, Italian-seasoned, herbed, spiced, Dutch-fried, cheesy, thick 'n crispy, or plump 'n juicy." They do it all for you.

The packages say, "For best results, conventional heating is recommended." However, we found the microwave-prepared product perfectly acceptable when heated according to the following directions.

Place a single layer of the frozen chicken product on a microwave-safe plate lined with paper towels. Do not cover. **MW on high** according to the recommended time for the particular product, turning each piece upside down midway through cooking.

Besides the typical breaded or fried chicken products, frozen chopped cooked chicken is available. One package is equivalent to the amount of meat from a deboned 3-lb fryer. It includes a mix of white and dark meat. It can be used in any recipe requiring cooked chicken meat.

CHICKEN THIGHS DIABLO

0.15	✳	399 cals

Serves 4

3 Tbsp soy sauce

4 tsp cornstarch

4 Tbsp dry sherry

1/2 tsp ground ginger

1/2 tsp minced garlic; or 1 clove garlic, minced

1/8 tsp cayenne pepper

2 lb chicken thighs

paprika

Whether you title this recipe Diablo, Lucifer, Beelzebub, or Mephistopheles, it's devilishly spicy but celestially good.

1 In an 8-in round or square baking dish, combine soy sauce and cornstarch. Stir well to smooth out all lumps. Stir in sherry, ginger, garlic, and cayenne pepper.

2 Rinse chicken in cool water and pat dry using paper towels. If you don't like chicken skin or you want to reduce calories, remove skin.

3 Place chicken in dish and coat each piece in soy sauce mixture. Arrange pieces skin side down, with the meaty portions toward the outside of dish. Cover with waxed paper and **MW on high** for 6 minutes.

4 Turn each piece over, keeping meaty portions toward the outside of dish. Stir sauce so that it will thicken evenly, and spoon sauce over chicken. Sprinkle with paprika. Re-cover and **MW on high** for 6 to 8 minutes.

5 Let chicken rest 5 minutes. Spoon sauce over chicken to serve.

Serving Suggestion
This simple chicken can be enhanced with a potato casserole, such as Haggerty (page 153), and either a green vegetable or salad.

A chilled Sauterne is a nice accompaniment. To follow this simple dinner, the rich Mandarin Cheese Pie (page 120) would make a delicious dessert.

LEFTOVERS

To freeze leftovers in individual portions for future use, put the desired amount of food into freezer-weight zip-locking bags. Label and freeze.

It is not necessary to defrost food before reheating it. Open about 1 in of bag seal so that steam can vent. Place frozen bag of food on a dinner plate. **MW on 70% (medium-high)** for about 3 minutes, or until hot enough to serve. Transfer to plate.

If you have a small appliance that seals meals in airtight plastic pouches, you can also freeze leftovers by this method.

PLAY CHICKEN WITH THE MICROWAVE... AND WIN!

If you remember "odds and ends," it's easy to microwave delicious chicken. Arrange assorted-shaped parts properly, with the ends in the center of a dish and the "odd man out."

Poultry is an especially good food to microwave because it is a tender meat, and it cooks beautifully on high power. To determine microwaving time, always weigh chicken on a scale. The greater the weight, the longer the microwave time needed. To determine cooking time on high power, multiply the weight of "bone-in" poultry times 6 to 7 minutes per pound. Boneless chicken will be done in 4 to 5 minutes per pound.

For chicken parts with a crispy texture, coat with cornflake crumbs or coating mix. Arrange on a bacon rack and cover with waxed paper. For chicken that will be eaten with a knife and fork, place in a baking dish with or without a sauce (such as Italian or barbecue sauce) and cover with plastic wrap, then microwave for required time.

WHAT IS A BREAST HALF?

The term "chicken breast half" may sound confusing. Chickens do not have 2 distinct breasts; a chicken breast is one continuous expanse that thins as it crosses the breastbone. When chickens are cut up and packaged for supermarket sales, chicken breasts are split down the breastbone. These are labelled "chicken breast halves."

If you have been served one of these chicken parts at dinner, you may have thought of it as a chicken breast. Technically, however, it is a breast half, the same part specified in a recipe. It does not mean to cut one of these in half again!

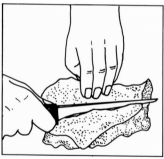

If you are cutting up a chicken at home, cut through the ribs to detach the breast from the chicken. Then cut the breast in half along the breastbone, leaving the breastbone attached to one of the halves.

CHICKEN BREASTS IN CHAMPAGNE

| 0.30 | 🍳 | $ | ✳ | * | 775 cals |

*freeze without sauce

Serves 4

| 1 package (6-oz) long-grain and wild rice mixed |
| 1 medium onion, sliced |
| 1 medium carrot, sliced |
| 1 bay leaf |
| 6 chicken breast halves, about 2½ to 3 lb |
| ¼ tsp ground ginger |
| 1 cup Champagne or dry white wine |
| Kitchen Bouquet |
| paprika |
| 1 cup heavy cream |
| 1 cup seedless green grapes, sliced in half |

1 Cook rice according to directions on page 155. Set aside.

2 Place onion and carrot slices on the bottom of a 2-qt rectangular glass dish. Add bay leaf.

3 Rinse chicken in cool water and pat dry using paper towels. Place chicken skin side down on top of vegetables. Arrange so that the meat is toward the outside of the dish and the rib bones are toward the center. Mix ginger into Champagne and pour over chicken. Do not cover. **MW on high** for 10 minutes.

4 Turn each piece over so that it is skin side up. Arrange as above. Rub skin with Kitchen Bouquet so that it looks light brown. Sprinkle with paprika. **MW on high** for 8 to 11 minutes.

5 Put cooked rice on a large platter. Remove chicken from dish and place on top of rice. Add grapes, spacing them around chicken to look attractive.

6 Remove onion and carrot slices from dish and save for another use. Add cream to Champagne in dish, then add salt and pepper to taste. **MW on high** until liquid just begins to boil.

7 Pour some sauce over the chicken and put remainder in a small pitcher to serve at the table. If there are any leftovers, the chicken and rice can be frozen. However, do not freeze the sauce or the grapes because the cream will curdle and the grapes will become mushy.

Serving Suggestion
Serve over Long Grain and Wild Rice (page 155), with a slightly sweet white wine, such as a Rhine from Germany.

Billy Graham's Missionary Chicken

| 0.25 | $ ✳ * | 365 cals |

*can freeze but vegetables will not stay crisp

Serves 4

1 small onion, sliced

1 cup diagonally sliced celery

1 red bell pepper, quartered, seeded, and sliced

2 Tbsp corn oil

1 lb boneless chicken breasts, thinly sliced

4 Tbsp soy sauce

1 clove garlic, minced

1 tsp ground ginger

1 can (8-oz) bamboo shoots, with liquid

2 Tbsp cornstarch

1 cup chicken broth

1 package (6-oz) frozen snow peas, defrosted (see note)

steamed rice (page 154)

1/2 cup toasted sliced almonds

When Dr. Graham sent us this recipe, it was titled "Jiffy Chicken." Since it was oriental in flavor, it made us think of what missionaries to China might cook with ingredients they found.

1 Put onion, celery, bell pepper, and oil in a 2-qt glass batter bowl. Cover with plastic wrap. **MW on high** for 4 to 5 minutes.

2 Using a slotted spoon, remove vegetables and set aside on a plate. To liquid remaining in bowl, add chicken, soy sauce, garlic, and ginger. Re-cover. **MW on high** for 2 minutes.

3 Stir chicken to separate slices. Re-cover and **MW on high** for 2 to 3 minutes. Using slotted spoon, remove chicken and set aside with vegetables.

4 Into a small mixing bowl, drain liquid from can of bamboo shoots. Stir cornstarch into liquid until mixture is smooth. Add to liquid remaining in batter bowl. Add chicken broth. **MW on high** for 2 to 3 minutes, or until liquid thickens.

5 Transfer cooked vegetables and chicken back into batter bowl. Add snow peas. **MW on high** to serving temperature. To serve, spoon over rice and top with toasted almonds.

Serving Suggestion
As appetizers before this main dish, serve purchased egg rolls or hot and sour soup. For a beverage, serve hot tea, warmed sake (white rice wine), or room temperature plum wine.

NOTE
To defrost snow peas, place package on a paper towel on floor of microwave oven. **MW on high** for 2 to 3 minutes.

BONING CHICKEN BREASTS

To "bone" means to separate the bones from meat. You can bone cooked or raw meat. Generally, once the bones have been removed from cooked meat, they have no further use and should be discarded. However, raw bones and the meat left on them can be stewed with water in a saucepan to make stock or broth.

Raw chicken breasts are probably the item which is boned most often. Several of the recipes in this book use boneless chicken breasts. You can purchase these already boned at the supermarket, but it is less expensive to buy chicken breasts and bone them yourself.

job — and other boning jobs — easier. However, boning can also be done with a sharp paring knife.

Whether you are boning a whole or half chicken breast, the procedure is the same. Begin at the breastbone, and cut along the bone and cartilage to free the meat. Cut and scrape the meat away from the bones, gently pulling back breast meat in one piece toward the rib edges as you cut.

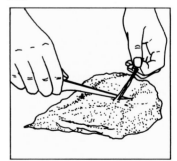

When meat is completely detached from bones, remove skin and cut out the white tendon. The boneless breast can be microwaved in one piece or cut into chunks according to the recipe.

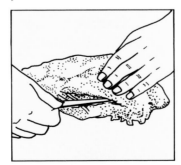

If you don't already have one, a boning knife makes this

BOB HOPE'S FAVORITE CHICKEN HASH

| 0.15 | ✳ | 455 cals |

Serves 2

2 chicken breast halves

2 strips bacon

2 green onions including tops, thinly sliced

2 Tbsp butter or margarine

4 Tbsp sour cream

1 tsp fresh lemon juice

2 tsp dry sherry

salt and black pepper to taste

1 Place chicken in a glass pie plate and cover with plastic wrap. **MW on high** for 6 to 7 minutes.

2 Take cooked chicken out of pie plate and put on a dinner plate to cool. Add green onions and butter to the juices left in the pie plate. Cover with same plastic wrap and **MW on high** for 2 minutes. Add sour cream, lemon juice, and sherry. Set aside.

3 Put a folded paper towel on a microwave-safe plate or paper plate. Place bacon on towel and cover with another paper towel. **MW on high** for 2 to 2 1/2 minutes, or until crisp. Remove bacon; cool and crumble.

4 Bone chicken. Discard skin and bones, and cut cooked meat into fine strips. Add chicken to sauce in plate. Stir to coat evenly. Add crumbled bacon. Reheat before serving; **MW on 70% (medium-high)** for 1 to 2 minutes.

Serving Suggestion
Nutmeg Spinach (page 153) would add color and zip to this entree. For dessert, try the Cherry Almond Pie (page 119).

WHY COOK?

It's good to have a little knowledge of cooking. Knowing about food adds glamor to a bachelor. For the man married to a non-cook, it means rescue when things begin to go black.

For the man whose wife is a good cook, it can be comforting to know he can go on munching while she's out of town. To the host, when the guys drop in for poker, it means you can stir up something in a jiffy.

Some wives have a whole shelf of cookbooks, filled with newspaper clippings, file cards, and scraps of paper. But those books are aimed at people who already know how to cook! Where do you look for an explanation of how to "fold in" an ingredient? Where does it explain how to separate eggs? The answers to these and many other cooking questions are in this book, directed toward the inexperienced cook, the man stepping into the kitchen for the first time.

15-MINUTE JAMBALAYA

| 0.30 | ✳ | 383 cals |

Serves 8

2 cloves garlic, peeled

2 ribs celery

1 medium onion, peeled

1 green bell pepper, seeded

1 cup cooked chicken

1 can (28-oz) tomatoes

1 can (14½-oz) chicken broth

3 Tbsp tomato paste

¼ tsp cayenne or red pepper

1 lb fully cooked link sausage

2½ cups instant rice

1 Mince garlic and chop celery, onion, and pepper by hand, or use a food processor. Transfer to a 4-qt pot. Cover. **MW on high** for 5 minutes.

2 Chop chicken into chunks by hand or use processor. Add chicken to pot.

3 Drain liquid from can of tomatoes into pot. Mash tomatoes with a fork or place in food processor and pulse until tomatoes are coarsely chopped. Add tomatoes, chicken broth, tomato paste, and cayenne pepper to pot.

4 Slice sausage by hand or insert slicing disk into food processor. Cut sausage crosswise to fit in feed tube. Using firm pressure, slice sausage and add to pot. Cover and **MW on high** for 10 minutes, or until liquid begins to boil.

5 Stir in instant rice, re-cover, and let stand 10 minutes, or until liquid is absorbed.

MICROWAVING A DUCK OR GOOSE

These birds have a high fat content. Microwave them in an oven cooking bag to make discarding fat easier and to ensure tender meat. To prepare for cooking, stuff goose or duck if desired. Tie bird compactly, using unwaxed dental floss or trussing string.

Poultry will not become acceptably brown during microwaving, so "cosmetics" must be applied. Rub the skin with a bottled brown sauce such as Kitchen Bouquet, or sprinkle with Micro Shake. Shield drumsticks and wings with aluminum foil.

Place bird in oven cooking bag, and weigh. Determine cooking time at 5 to 6 minutes per pound on high power. Set bird in a rectangular baking dish. Tie end of cooking bag loosely with a strip of plastic wrap, string, or dental floss. Begin cooking breast side down. After half of cooking time, pour off fat and turn bird breast side up. Microwave for remaining cooking time, pour off fat again, and let stand 10 minutes before carving.

ROAST DUCKLING WITH LEMON SAUCE

| 0.40 | $$ ✳ * | 698 cals |

*freeze without sauce

Serves 4

1 domestic duckling, 4 to 5 lb, thawed

1 lemon

Micro Shake or Kitchen Bouquet

2 tsp cornstarch

1 tsp sugar

1 tsp instant chicken bouillon granules

dash of cayenne pepper

½ cup fresh or defrosted frozen lemon juice

½ cup hot tap water

1 large egg

1 Duckling must be completely thawed so that it will cook evenly. Remove neck and giblets and save for another use. Wash duck inside and out, and pat dry.

2 Using a cooking fork, pierce skin at intervals on all sides of duck so that fat can drip out. Tie legs and wings close to body of duck using trussing string or unwaxed dental floss. Squeeze juice from lemon over skin of duck.

3 Sprinkle duck generously with Micro Shake, or rub with 1 tsp of Kitchen Bouquet. Shield wings and drumsticks with pieces of aluminum foil. Place prepared duck in a large-size oven cooking bag. Tie end loosely with a strip of plastic wrap, string, or dental floss. Weigh duck and determine cooking time at 5 to 6 minutes per pound on high power.

4 Place duck breast side down in a 2-qt rectangular dish. Microwave for half the determined cooking time. Pour off fat that has accumulated. Turn duck breast side up, re-close bag, and microwave for remaining cooking time. Pour off fat and let stand 10 minutes before carving.

5 Meanwhile, prepare lemon sauce. Combine cornstarch, sugar, instant bouillon, and cayenne in a 1-qt glass measure. Using a whisk, blend in lemon juice. Whisk in water and egg. Whisking every 2 minutes, **MW on high** for 5 to 6 minutes, or until sauce is thickened. Serve hot in a pitcher with carved duckling.

Serving Suggestion
This rather rich entree would go nicely with a light vegetable accompaniment, such as a casserole of summer squash. Serve with a chilled dry white wine. For a light dessert, top some vanilla ice cream with Chocolate Kahlua Sauce (page 157).

MICRO SHAKE

Micro Shake was developed by Dr. Ghazi Taki. Consisting of all-natural ingredients, this mixture helps to brown and tenderize meats during microwaving. It is available in regular and salt-free versions of both chicken and beef flavors. Moisten uncooked meat and sprinkle liberally with Micro Shake.

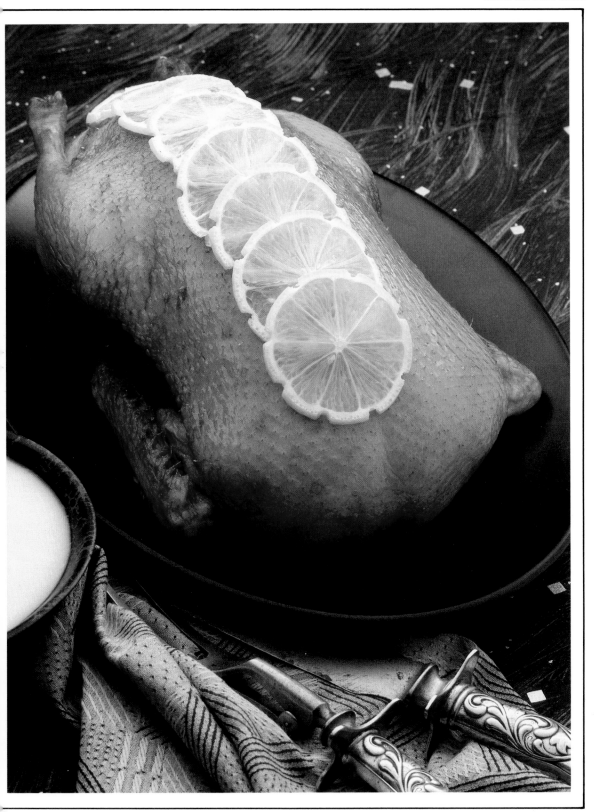

ED McMAHON'S ROAST TURKEY WITH DRESSING

| 1.30 | 🗋 ✳ | 639 cals |

Serves 12

1 bag (8-oz) herb-seasoned stuffing mix

1 bag (8-oz) cornbread stuffing mix

8 oz bulk country sausage

1 cup chopped onions

1 cup chopped celery

1 can (4-oz) mushroom pieces, drained

1 cup apple sauce

1 can (8-oz) crushed pineapple, with liquid

³/₄ cup brandy

¹/₂ cup chopped walnuts

4 Tbsp orange marmalade

1 turkey, 11 to 15 lb, thawed

2 tsp Kitchen Bouquet

2 tsp oil

paprika

1 Combine the stuffing mixes in a large mixing bowl. Set aside. Crumble sausage into a 1-qt glass measure. Add onions and celery and **MW on high** for 3 minutes.

2 Stir to combine mixture, then **MW on high** for 2 to 3 minutes more, or until sausage is no longer pink.

3 Drain grease into a can to discard later. Stir sausage to break up chunks and transfer sausage mixture to bowl containing stuffing mix. Add mushroom pieces, apple sauce, pineapple including liquid, brandy, walnuts, and marmalade. Stir well.

4 If turkey has a metal clamp securing drumsticks, remove it. Stuff turkey. Mix Kitchen Bouquet and oil together and brush mixture all over turkey. Sprinkle with paprika.

5 Use aluminum foil to shield wings and drumstick ends. Using unwaxed dental floss or string, tie wings close to body of turkey, and tie drumsticks together. Place turkey in an extra-large oven cooking bag and weigh stuffed (or unstuffed, if desired). To determine microwaving time, multiply the weight by 6 to 7 minutes per pound.

6 Set turkey in bag breast side down in a 2-qt rectangular dish. Tear a 2-in strip from a roll of plastic wrap and use it to tie end of bag loosely, leaving an opening the size of a quarter for a steam vent. **MW on high** for half the cooking time you determined.

7 Pour juices which have accumulated in bag into a large measuring cup. Turn turkey breast side up. Brush with more Kitchen Bouquet and sprinkle with paprika if additional color is needed. **MW on high** for remaining cooking time. At the end of cooking, pour off juices again, and let turkey stand in bag for 20 minutes. The internal temperature of turkey should be 180°F. after standing time.

8 Spoon out stuffing, then carve turkey. Serve hot.

Serving Suggestion

Baked acorn squash makes a perfect taste combination with turkey. Serve with a slightly sweet white wine such as one from the Mosel in Germany.

CARVING A TURKEY

Have the heat on a very large platter, or have an extra place nearby for holding the carved meat. Take your best golf stance and start cutting.

Insert fork into top of breast. Slice down through joint where legs join cavity.

Slice down where wings attach to cavity.

Slice down from breast tip at an angle that follows the curve in cavity.

Meat on the Hoof

Beef, veal, pork, and lamb can all emerge from the microwave oven tender and delicious if the correct power level and cooking techniques are used. Broadly speaking, all meat is divided into 2 classes: tender and tough. It makes little difference whether it was formerly Army, Navy, or Air Force. But if it was some kind of Marine, it will take longer cooking on a lower power level to make it tender!

ROLLED STUFFED STEAK

| 0.25 | ✳ | 512 cals |

Serves 4

1 flank steak, about 1¹⁄₃ to 1¹⁄₂ lb

meat tenderizer or beef-flavor Micro Shake

6 slices bacon

¹⁄₂ lb fresh mushrooms, sliced

2 Tbsp margarine or butter

¹⁄₂ cup dry stuffing mix

garlic powder

salt and black pepper

2 tsp Worcestershire sauce

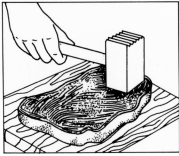

1 Use a wooden mallet or rolling pin to pound steak evenly to a ¹⁄₂-in thickness.

2 Use a sharp carving knife to make shallow cuts diagonally across the opposite direction from first side. Sprinkle both sides of steak with meat tenderizer or Micro Shake. Set aside.

3 Put a paper towel on your microwave bacon rack. Separate strips of bacon and arrange on paper towel. Cover with another paper towel. **MW on high** for 5 minutes, or until almost done but not crisp. Peel bacon off paper towel and set aside.

4 Place mushrooms and margarine in a 4-cup glass measure. Cover with plastic wrap and **MW on high** for 3 to 4 minutes.

5 Stir stuffing into mushroom mixture until liquid is absorbed. Sprinkle steak with garlic powder, salt, and pepper. Spread stuffing mixture evenly over surface of steak. Lay strips of bacon across stuffing. Beginning with thick end, roll up steak, making sure that stuffing is enclosed. Use string or unwaxed dental floss to tie around roll in several places.

6 Place rolled steak in a baking dish and sprinkle with Worcestershire sauce. Cover with waxed paper. Turning steak over a quarter of a turn every 2 minutes, **MW on high** for 6 to 8 minutes. Baste with juices. To serve, remove string and cut into ¹⁄₂-in slices.

Serving Suggestion

A hearty potato casserole, such as Hot Tomato Potatoes (page 154) would taste great with beef. Serve with a red Bordeaux wine.

STANDING RIB ROAST WITH YORKSHIRE PUDDING

| 2.00 | $$ ✳ | 752 cals |

1 standing rib roast, small end preferred (allow ½ lb per person)

3 cloves garlic, peeled and cut in half

Micro Shake or Kitchen Bouquet

selected herbs (rosemary, thyme, parsley, dill, etc.)

1 Rub meat with garlic. Make 6 small slits in fat pockets or near rib bones and insert cut garlic. If using Micro Shake, moisten roast with water and then sprinkle it on. If using Kitchen Bouquet, wipe it all over dry roast. Sprinkle roast with your favorite herbs.

2 Place roast on a microwave meat rack, with either of its flat ends facing up. If using a temperature probe, insert point horizontally into the center of the meat halfway between the 2 ends of the roast. Make sure that the probe is not resting on bone or fat.

3 Tear a 20-in length from a roll of waxed paper. Fold paper in half crosswise and drape it over the roast with the fold at the top. This makes a tent to hold in the heat. Program your temperature probe according to desired doneness (see right). **MW on high** for 5 minutes.

4 Remove the tent and turn roast top to bottom. Replace tent and **MW on 50% (medium)** for half of the cooking time as given below (or until temperature probe reads 110°). Turn roast bone side down and replace tent. Microwave for remainder of cooking time. Remove roast from oven and cover with tent of aluminum foil. Let stand 10 to 15 minutes.

Serving Suggestion
This simple but hearty British meal would be complete with the addition of Bleu Ribbon Broccoli (page 150). Serve with a hearty red Burgundy. For dessert, Chocolate Mocha Mousse (page 125) would be light on the palate.

TIMING CHART

Internal Temperature		Minutes per pound on 50%
Rare	120°F.	11 to 13
Medium	130°F.	13 to 15
Well Done	150°F.	15 to 17

NOTE
Temperature of roast will rise 15°F. additionally after microwaving while roast is standing.

SKIMMING THE FAT
If you have plenty of time, the best way to remove fat from meat juices is to pour the cooking liquid into a tall, narrow glass jar and refrigerate it. The fat will become solid and can be scooped off the top with a spoon.

If you don't have time to chill the cooking liquid, pour it into the jar and watch for the layer of fat to concentrate at the top, then spoon it off.

It is more difficult to skim fat from a wide, shallow pan (such as a roasting pan), because the fat layer is thin and you will also remove the valuable juices along with the fat. Rather, drag strips of paper towel over the surface to absorb the fat.

CARVING A RIB ROAST
Place the cooked roast on a carving platter or cutting board. If you are right handed, put the flat side of the roast facing down with the rib

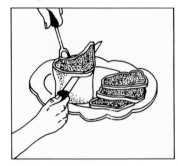

toward the top rib bone, making a slice no more than ½ in thick.

Pull knife out. Use tip of knife to cut down along rib bone deep enough to release first slice. Place carved meat on a warmed dinner plate.

Continue carving slices, cutting under and removing each rib bone as it becomes exposed.

bones at your left. Left-handers should do the opposite. Hold roast by placing carving fork between rib bones. With the carving knife, cut across the meat

INDIVIDUAL YORKSHIRE PUDDINGS

Makes 12

beef drippings

1 cup milk

2 large eggs

1 cup all-purpose flour

½ tsp salt

1 Move shelf in conventional oven to middle position. Preheat oven to 450° F. Spoon about ½ tsp of drippings from roast into each of the 12 compartments of a metal muffin pan. Place pan in oven for 5 minutes.

2 While pan is heating, pour milk into a 4-cup glass measure to the 1-cup mark. Crack the eggs into the milk and beat well. Stir flour and salt into egg mixture and beat until well blended.

3 Ladle the batter into each compartment of heated muffin pan, using a ¼-cup measure about ¾'s full of batter. Bake 10 minutes; do not open the oven door. Reduce the oven temperature to 350° and continue to bake about 15 minutes, or until puddings are puffy and brown.

4 While puddings are baking, microwave vegetables to accompany your dinner, and carve roast.

WESTFALISCHER SHORTRIBS WITH LEMON-CAPER SAUCE

1.45	✳	571 cals

Serves 4

coarsely ground black pepper

2 lb beef shortribs, cut into 2-in sections

4 cups thinly sliced onions

2 cups boiling water

2 tsp instant beef bouillon granules

1 bay leaf

¼ tsp ground cloves

1 slice fresh pumpernickel bread

2 Tbsp fresh lemon juice

½ tsp finely grated lemon peel

2 tsp drained capers

1 Soak bottom and lid of a microwave-safe clay roasting pan in tap water for 15 minutes. Meanwhile, pepper shortribs generously and rub into meat. Brown ribs in a skillet on top of stove, using a small amount of oil. Transfer ribs to bottom of clay pot, placing meaty sides toward the outer edges of pot.

2 Put onions into a 4-cup glass measure. Cover with plastic wrap and **MW on high** for 6 to 7 minutes.

3 Add onions to ribs. Pour boiling water over onions and ribs. Add bouillon, bay leaf, and cloves. Cover with lid. **MW on high** for 20 minutes.

4 Turn each rib over and exchange ribs in the center of the dish for ribs at the outer edges. Re-cover and **MW on 50% (medium)** for 30 minutes.

5 Rearrange ribs as above. Re-cover and **MW on 50%** for another 30 minutes, or until tender. Remove cooked ribs to a warm platter.

6 Using food processor or blender, make fine crumbs from bread slice. Stir crumbs, lemon juice, and lemon peel into mixture remaining in pot. Rinse capers in cold water; add to pot. **MW on high** until mixture boils. Remove bay leaf and discard. Taste a spoonful for seasoning. The sauce should be peppery.

NOTE

Unglazed terracotta pots by Litton, Nordic Ware, and Romertopf are safe to use in both microwave and conventional ovens. If you have a clay pot and are not sure if it is safe to use in your microwave, test it first. Place the dry pot in the microwave oven next to a 1-cup measure of water. **MW on high** 1 minute 15 seconds. If the pot is cool and the water warm, it is microwave safe.

Soak the pot — both bottom and lid — for 15 minutes in cold tap water while you prepare the ingredients for your recipe.

Drain water from pot bottom and place ingredients in. Arrange the larger pieces of food around the outside of the pot, and put small pieces in the center. Foods around the outside will get more microwaves. If adding salt, dissolve it in the cooking liquid. Do not sprinkle salt directly onto the surface of foods because it will toughen them.

Drain water from the pot lid and fit in place over food. Do not slide the clay pot into the microwave oven because the unglazed clay might scratch the bottom of your oven. **MW on high** for 15 minutes to activate the water molecules in the clay so they begin steaming. For beef or pork, reduce power to 50% for subsequent cooking time. Poultry can be microwaved entirely on high.

CAJUN MEATLOAF

0.15 ✳ 361 cals

Serves 4

½ cup chopped onion

½ cup chopped green bell pepper

2 green onions and tops, thinly sliced

1 large clove garlic, minced

2 tsp Worcestershire sauce

1½ tsp Tabasco sauce

1 tsp salt

½ tsp cayenne pepper

½ tsp black pepper

¼ tsp white pepper

½ tsp ground cumin

¼ tsp ground nutmeg

1 bay leaf

4 Tbsp (¼ cup) evaporated milk

4 Tbsp (¼ cup) ketchup

1 large egg, lightly beaten

1 lb ground beef

½ cup dry bread crumbs

1 In a 2-qt glass batter bowl, combine onion, green pepper, green onions, garlic, Worcestershire, Tabasco, salt, cayenne, black pepper, white pepper, cumin, nutmeg, and bay leaf. Cover with plastic wrap. **MW on high** for 3 minutes.

2 Remove bay leaf and add milk and ketchup. Beat in egg. Stir in ground beef and bread crumbs. (Mixing with hands works best!) Form mixture into a rectangular loaf and place on a microwave bacon rack. Cover with waxed paper. Turning rack halfway around after 5 minutes, **MW on 70% (medium-high)** for 10 to 12 minutes. Let stand 10 minutes before slicing.

Serving Suggestion

Jalapeño Cheese Grits (page 155) make a Gulf Coast partnership with this Creole entree. Serve with a Beaujolais wine. For dessert, cool off with Bill Rodgers' Blueberry Crisp (page 127) served over ice cream.

CAJUN AND CREOLE COOKING

Classic New Orleans cooking, which is one of the most distinctive regional cuisines in America, originated with Creole and Cajun cooks. They took French cooking techniques and traditional English recipes and adapted them to the new seasonings and ingredients that were brought in by the Spanish, Indian, and African workers.

Creole is the French equivalent for the Spanish *criollo* — the Spanish or French descendants who were born in the colonies. *Cajun* refers to the French-speaking refugees who fled in 1755, to Southwest Louisiana from Acadia, Nova Scotia, after the British invasion.

There is some controversy about the distinctions between Creole and Cajun cooking. Generally, Creole cooking is closer to classic French cuisine, with its delicate blends and subtle sauces. Cajun, on the other hand, derives from a more rustic country-style cooking, using similar ingredients, but in a rougher form.

THE BETTER MEATLOAF

In just 10 to 12 minutes, you can microwave a delicious meatloaf. In the same length of time, you can also ruin a meatloaf! There are a few quirky things about microwaving them. If you keep these in mind, you will have a better meatloaf.

If chopped raw vegetables (such as onions, celery, or bell pepper) are combined with raw meat, they will stay crunchy after the meatloaf is cooked. Microwave the chopped vegetables in a measuring cup before adding them to the raw meat mixture (unless you particularly like crisp vegetables in your meatloaf!).

Meatloaves will shrink less if you microwave them on 70% (medium-high) instead of high. Shape them into a rectangular loaf rather than a wide round loaf. (A rectangular loaf gets done in the center faster.) Shield the ends of the loaf with aluminum foil if they appear to be overcooking. Cook the meatloaf on a bacon rack so that the fat can drain off as it microwaves. Keep it covered with waxed paper during cooking to hold in the heat.

If you want to double a meatloaf recipe, shape it into a large doughnut so that it will microwave evenly. Let the meatloaf stand after microwaving for at least half the original cooking time. This standing allows it to finish cooking, and the loaf will hold together better for slicing.

MEATBALL STROGANOFF

0.25	534 cals

Serves 4

1 lb ground beef

1 large egg

1 slice bread, crumbed

1 tsp salt

¼ tsp black pepper

1 large onion, chopped

8 oz fresh mushrooms, sliced

3 Tbsp margarine or butter

3 Tbsp all-purpose flour

2 Tbsp fresh lemon juice

1 Tbsp Worcestershire sauce

1 Tbsp ketchup

1 cup beef bouillon

4 Tbsp (¼ cup) red wine

1 cup sour cream

1 Place 3 paper towels in the bottom of a 2-qt rectangular dish. In a medium bowl, mix ground beef, egg, bread crumbs, salt, and pepper. Form meat mixture into 1-in balls, and place in a single layer on paper towels. Cover with another paper towel. **MW on high** for 3 minutes.

2 Exchange places of the most-done meatballs on sides with those in center least done. **MW on high** for 2 to 3 minutes.

3 Place onion, mushrooms, and margarine in a 2-qt casserole. Cover with lid or plastic wrap. **MW on high** for 3 minutes.

4 Stir flour into onion mixture. Add lemon juice, Worcestershire, ketchup, bouillon, and wine. **MW on high** for 6 minutes, stirring midway through cooking.

5 Transfer cooked meatballs to sauce mixture. Fold in sour cream. Just before serving, reheat on 70% (medium-high).

Serving Suggestion

Serve over cooked noodles or rice. Garnish with chopped fresh parsley. Serve Continental Brussels Sprouts (page 151), with a light red wine.

SOUR CREAM

Commercial, or "dairy," sour cream is made from light rather than heavy cream and averages only about 30 calories per tablespoon. When purchasing sour cream, read the expiration date on the carton to be sure that it is fresh. Once opened, a carton of sour cream will last up to 10 days in the refrigerator. If a watery liquid appears above the sour cream, it is not spoiled; stir the mixture before using to combine again. Sour cream cannot be frozen because it will curdle and separate.

MUSHROOMS

When purchasing fresh button mushrooms, select those with firm white caps and beige stems. No gills should be showing where the caps join the stems, and the mushrooms should not have bruises.

Before cooking, store mushrooms in the refrigerator in their original store packaging, punctured open, or cover them loosely with a barely damp paper towel so that air can circulate around them. Since mushrooms bruise easily, do not stack other foods on top of them. Use fresh mushrooms raw in salads or cook them only briefly. Use fresh mushrooms within a few days.

To prepare mushrooms for cooking, do not peel them or soak in water. Wipe each mushroom gently with a barely wet paper towel. Cut a

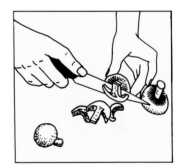

thin slice off bottom of stems and discard. Slice mushrooms parallel to the stem or leave whole. Microwave as recipe directs.

Cooked mushrooms can be kept in the refrigerator 4 to 5 days, or can be frozen for up to a year. Do not freeze raw mushrooms because they will be mushy after defrosting.

PAT BOONE'S SPAGHETTI WESTERN

| 0.40 | ❋ * | 713 cals |

*freeze without sauce

Serves 4

1 lb ground beef or raw turkey

1 medium onion, chopped

1 to 2 Tbsp chili powder

1 tsp dried basil

¾ tsp garlic powder

1 can (28-oz) tomatoes, with liquid

1 can (6-oz) tomato paste

4 oz vermicelli (thin spaghetti)

1 can (16-oz) red kidney beans, drained

1 cup shredded sharp Cheddar cheese

1 cup sour cream

The title of this favorite recipe of singer/movie star Pat Boone refers to a phrase used in the movie industry, which means a cowboy movie filmed in Italy.

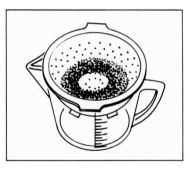

1 Place a dishwasher-safe plastic colander in a 4-qt pot. Crumble ground meat into colander and sprinkle onion on top. **MW on high** for 3 minutes.

2 Use a wooden spoon to stir meat and break up chunks. **MW on high** for 3 minutes, or until meat is no longer pink; stir. Pour grease into a can to discard later.

3 Transfer meat to pot. Stir in chili powder, basil, and ½ tsp garlic powder. Pour liquid from tomatoes into pot, then coarsely chop tomatoes, using a knife or food processor and then add to pot. Stir in tomato paste. Fill paste can with water and add. Cover with lid or plastic wrap. **MW on high** for 10 minutes, or until bubbly hot.

4 Break spaghetti into 2-in pieces and stir into meat mixture. Re-cover and **MW on high** for 6 minutes.

5 Stir to redistribute spaghetti, re-cover and **MW on high** for 3 to 4 minutes, or until spaghetti is tender.

6 Add beans to spaghetti mixture, cover, and let stand 5 minutes.

7 Combine cheese, sour cream, and remaining garlic powder in a 2-cup glass measure. **MW on 70% (medium-high)** for 2 minutes; stir. Microwave longer if cheese has not melted. Reheat spaghetti on high if necessary. Top servings with cheese sauce.

NOTE

Leftover Spaghetti Western freezes well. Do not top with cheese sauce if freezing because it will curdle and separate.

Serving Suggestion

For this pasta dish, add a simple green vegetable, such as Nutmeg Spinach (page 153). Serve with a red Bardolino wine.

DEFROSTING GROUND MEATS

When you arrive home from the store with packages of ground beef, don't just throw them into the freezer. A "brick" of ground meat takes a long time to defrost. Instead, form the meat into 1-lb "doughnuts," wrap tightly, then freeze. They will defrost faster than a solid piece because there is no thick center.

If you plan to have hamburgers, form some of the meat into patties and stack them between layers of waxed paper. Put the stack into a plastic bag for freezing. (See page 141 for more information about hamburgers.)

To microwave defrost a "doughnut" of ground beef, remove it from its freezer packaging and place it in the dish you plan to use for your recipe. **MW on high** for 1 minute. Remove it from the microwave, and use a fork to scrape off the thawed portions onto a piece of waxed paper. Return the frozen portion to the microwave and **MW on high** for 1 minute. Repeat scraping and microwaving until all meat is defrosted. Proceed with recipe.

PORTUGUESE PORK WITH LEMON

| 0.12 | ✳ | 144 cals |

Serves 4

1 lb pork tenderloin, cut in 1-in cubes

¹/₂ tsp ground cumin

¹/₂ tsp ground coriander

¹/₂ tsp salt

1 Tbsp cornstarch

¹/₂ cup Portuguese rosé or white wine

¹/₂ tsp minced garlic

¹/₄ tsp Tabasco sauce

5 lemon slices, cut in half

paprika

2 Tbsp chopped fresh coriander or parsley

steamed rice (page 154)

1 Place pork in a 2-qt round casserole. Sprinkle with cumin, coriander, and salt. Toss to coat evenly.

2 Stir in cornstarch. Add wine, garlic, Tabasco, and lemon slices; stir. **MW on 70% (medium-high)** for 4 minutes.

3 Stir to redistribute pork and sauce. **MW on 70%** for 3 to 4 minutes, or until pork is no longer pink. Stir.

4 Sprinkle with paprika and fresh coriander. Serve over rice.

Serving Suggestion
Artichokes (page 149) would complement this Mediterranean recipe. Serve a chilled Portuguese rosé wine with dinner, and microwave David Clifford's French Coconut Pie (page 116) for dessert.

HOW CHOPPED IS CHOPPED?

The ingredients in a recipe should be chopped to the correct size. Pieces that are larger or smaller than specified will not cook in the same time called for in the recipe. Use these actual-size illustrations to gauge the proper size ingredients you need.

Diced

Chopped

Finely Chopped

Minced

MICROWAVING PORK

It has been proved that pork prepared in the microwave oven is safe, tender, juicy, and flavorful. The research was performed at Iowa State University and Gerling Laboratories, Modesto, California, and coordinated by the Pork Industry Group of the Meat Board.

As with conventional cooking, pork should be microwaved until no longer pink. If you plan to microwave the pork in an oven cooking bag, freeze the roast in the bag so it is ready for cooking after it defrosts. Once a pork roast is defrosted, do not refreeze unless you cook it first.

When freezing uncooked pork for future microwave defrosting, arrange the meat in the package to speed both the freezing and thawing processes. Re-package pork chops in a single layer, which will defrost much faster than a stack of solidly frozen chops. Arrange ground pork in a doughnut shape; the round shape and space in the center will allow more microwave penetration and will speed defrosting.

TERIYAKI CHOPSTICKS

| 0.15 | ✳ | 178 cals |

* plus marinating time

Serves 4

1¼ lb pork tenderloin

½ cup soy sauce

1 Tbsp sugar

½ tsp ground ginger or 1½ tsp minced fresh ginger

¼ tsp instant minced garlic

chopped fresh parsley

2 green onions, tops sliced

1 Cut pork into ¾-in cubes. In a mixing bowl, combine soy sauce, sugar, ginger, and garlic. Add pork cubes and let marinate at room temperature for 15 to 20 minutes.

2 Drain pork and reserve marinade. Thread cubes on bamboo skewers, leaving ¼-in between each piece. Place skewers on a bacon rack or in a 2-qt rectangular glass dish. Cover with waxed paper. Use marinade to baste skewers during cooking.

3 Rearranging position of skewers midway through cooking, **MW on 70% (medium-high)** for 8 to 10 minutes, or until no longer pink. Baste again with marinade. Garnish with chopped parsley or sliced green onion tops.

Serving Suggestion
Serve with Pepper Rice (page 155). Warmed sake or room temperature plum wine would be an appropriate beverage.

GINGER

Probably best known as the flavoring in gingerale, ginger root was also considered a medicine for several centuries. As a spice, ginger originated in Southeast Asia, and was used in China and India long before Marco Polo wrote of seeing Chinese ginger plantations on his 13th century travels. King Henry VIII recommended using ginger as a remedy for the plague, and it was also said that ginger cured the lovesick and prolonged life.

Dried ginger is ground from the root of the plant. Ginger root is also crystallized, preserved, and used fresh. Both dried and fresh ginger are sold at most supermarkets. They are not usually considered interchangeable.

ENTERTAINING

Aside from the obvious use of your microwave oven for fast cooking, you can find it helpful for entertaining in other ways.

Heat microwave-safe dinner plates, for example. Sprinkle each plate with a teaspoon of water and stack up. Place the stack on the floor of your oven and **MW on high** for 1 minute per plate. Wipe the water from the heated plates and serve.

Pamper your guests with steamed towels after dinner. Immerse fingertip towels in lemon water and squeeze out excess water. Roll each individually and place on a microwave-safe tray. **MW on high** for 20 to 25 seconds per towel.

BAKED HAM

2.00*	✳	198 cals

*depending on size

Serves 12

1 smoked ham portion with bone, 7 to 8 lb

¼ cup packed light brown sugar

2 Tbsp Dijon-style mustard

¼ tsp ground cloves

whole cloves

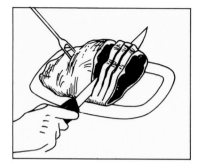

1 Remove rind from ham and place fat side down in an oven cooking bag. Shield top cut edge of ham with a 1½-in strip of foil, then close bag as package directs. Place ham in a baking dish.

2 If using a temperature probe, insert into center of meat, making sure that it does not touch bone. Plug probe into microwave oven and set for 160°F. on 50% (medium). When internal temperature of ham reaches 120°F., remove probe, pour off accumulated juices, and turn ham upside down.

3 Combine brown sugar, mustard, and ground cloves in a bowl. Glaze cut side of ham, then decorate top of ham with whole cloves.

4 Re-insert probe if using, then replace aluminum foil strip over top cut edge of ham and reclose bag. Continue to microwave until ham reaches proper internal temperature, or until cooking time is up. If not using temperature probe, **MW on 50% (medium) for 12 to 15 minutes per pound.** Midway through cooking, turn ham upside down. Let stand 15 minutes before carving. When ready, slice ham and serve.

Serving Suggestion
Nothing could be better than ham with Bourbon Yams (page 154) and an apple Waldorf salad. Serve with a chilled sparkling rosé wine with dinner.

NOTE
The Eastern part of mainland Virginia bordering the Chesapeake Bay is known as the Tidewater. This area is famous for its hams, especially the Smithfield ham. These dry-cured, smoked country hams must be soaked in water for several hours to extract the salt before baking.

Use a temperature probe to ensure that your ham is fully cooked. Fully cooked boneless hams should be microwaved to an internal temperature of 130 to 140°F. "Cook-before-eating" smoked hams with a bone must be microwaved to 160°F. When you insert the temperature probe, be certain the tip is resting in the center of the meat and not touching a bone.

DRYING HERBS

Fresh herbs (such as mint, dill, and parsley) will stay fresh in the refrigerator for only a few days. But by drying them in the microwave oven, you can preserve these herbs so that you have them to use months later.

While still fresh and bright, wash and blot them thoroughly with paper towels. Let them air-dry in the kitchen for several hours, because if any moisture remains on them when you dry them in the microwave, they will cook instead of dehydrating.

Put 3 paper towels on a glass pie plate. Arrange about 5 sprigs of herbs into a "wreath" on the towels. Do not remove the leaves from their stems. Cover herbs with another paper towel. **MW on high** for 1 minute.

Turn plate halfway around and look at herbs to see how dry they are becoming. **MW on high** for 1 minute and look at herbs again. If herbs are not dry, **MW on high** for 1 minute.

It is possible for dry herbs to catch on fire if you microwave them too long, so take them out of the microwave when they no longer feel soft to the touch. Let dried herbs cool. Then crumble leaves from stems and store them in an airtight jar. Use in any recipe specifying the amount in dried form.

MARINATED LOIN LAMB CHOPS

$0.16*$	$$ ✳	643 cals

*plus marinating time

Serves 2

2 Tbsp dry white wine

2 Tbsp corn oil

1 Tbsp fresh lemon juice

1 tsp Worcestershire sauce

1 tsp dried mint

$1/2$ tsp sugar

$1/4$ tsp minced garlic

$1/4$ tsp salt

dash of Tabasco sauce

4 loin lamb chops, about 1 lb

1 In a glass pie pan, mix wine, oil, lemon juice, Worcestershire, mint, sugar, garlic, salt, and Tabasco. Add lamb chops to marinade and turn to coat both sides. Place in refrigerator to marinate for 1 hour, turning chops over after 30 minutes.

2 Arrange lamb chops in pie pan so that meatier portions are toward the outside of the dish. Cover with waxed paper. Turning chops over after half of cooking, **MW on 70%** for 9 to 11 minutes, depending on desired doneness. Serve with mint jelly.

Serving Suggestion
A green vegetable, such as Crunchy Peas (page 152) will make a pretty plate. Serve dinner with a light red wine, such as a Bordeaux-Medoc. This simple dinner can precede a rich dessert, such as Jamocha Pecan Pie (page 114).

Campfires

Man's domain has always been the outdoor grill. We think there are many foods which taste best only when cooked over a fire, but you can use the microwave to improve the quality of your grilled foods. Microwave chicken, spareribs, and other items to partial doneness before putting them on the grill, thus cooking them to perfection. Also use your oven to reheat leftover barbecued foods. Even on rainy days, their outdoor flavor can be enjoyed again.

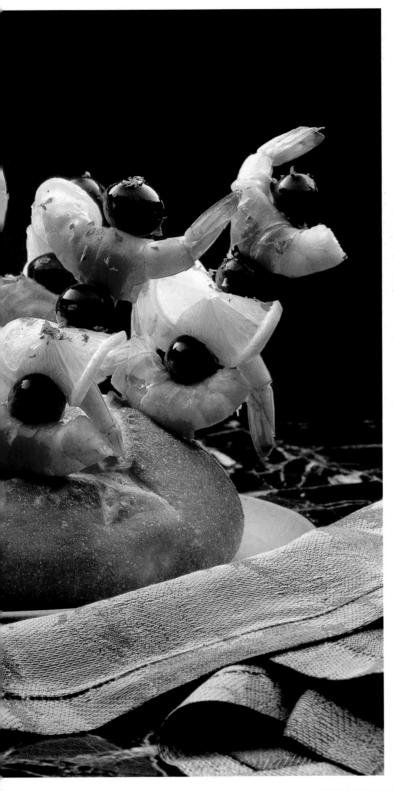

BARBECUED SHRIMP

0.35^* 🍴 $ $ 286 cals

*plus marinating time

Serves 4

5 Tbsp corn oil

1 lb shrimp in the shell

2 medium lemons

4 thin slices prosciutto

18 pitted black olives

4 Tbsp fresh lemon juice

4 Tbsp dry white wine

2 Tbsp Worcestershire sauce

2 Tbsp soy sauce

1/3 cup chopped fresh parsley

1/4 tsp crushed dried red pepper

salt and black pepper to taste

1 Using a small amount of oil, grease eight 6-in bamboo skewers so that they will be easier to push through the food. Leave tails on shrimp, but remove shell. Devein according to directions on page 41.

2 Cut lemons crosswise so that you have 12 slices.

3 Cut prosciutto into 3 strips each. Wrap half the shrimp with strips of prosciutto and wrap a lemon slice around the remaining shrimp.

4 Thread the 2 types of wrapped shrimp alternately with the olives on skewers. Place in a 2-qt rectangular glass dish.

5 In a 2-cup glass measure, combine lemon juice, wine, remaining oil, Worcestershire sauce, and soy sauce. Mix well. Add parsley, red pepper, and salt and pepper to taste. Stir and pour mixture over skewers of shrimp. Cover and refrigerate 1 hour.

6 Grill shrimp outdoors to desired doneness or **MW on high** for 30 to 40 seconds per skewer. Rearrange skewers midway through cooking.

MICROWAVE TO GRILL

Perfect outdoor grilling begins with a microwave oven! If you partially cook foods in the microwave before grilling them, they'll never be burned on the outside and raw in the center.

Arrange the foods in a microwave-safe pan with the thicker parts toward the outside of the dish and the thinner or bony areas in the center. Cover with waxed paper. For best results, microwave the food just before putting it on the grill so that it will stay hot and cook continuously.

Precook chicken, Cornish hens, turkey, roasts, and spareribs for 5 minutes per pound on high power, turning top to bottom midway through cooking. Pour off accumulated juices so that when you place the meat on the grill you won't put out the fire!

Since foods will be almost done after microwaving, they will be finished on the grill when they look beautifully brown. Remove one portion from grill and test for doneness.

Steaks, shish kabobs, and hamburger patties do not need pre-cooking. However, if you want to be fuel efficient, grill extras while the coals are still hot. Undercook them slightly, let cool, and then freezer wrap. Frozen grilled foods can be defrosted and reheated in the microwave oven at a later date, and they will taste like they were just grilled. Remove freezer wrappings and **MW on 70% (medium-high)** until defrosted and desired serving temperature.

To test whether your charcoal fire or gas grill is ready for the food, hold your hand over the fire at the same level the meat will be placed for cooking. Count the number of seconds you can comfortably keep your hand there. One or 2 seconds is a hot fire (good for steaks, burgers, and shish kabobs). Three or 4 seconds is a medium fire (good for chicken, Cornish hens, and spareribs). Five or 6 seconds is a slow fire (good for turkeys and roasts).

TANDOORI CHICKEN

0.40*	✳	435 cals

*plus marinating time

Serves 4

1 cup plain yogurt

3 Tbsp fresh lime or lemon juice

2 tsp minced garlic

2 tsp ground coriander

1 tsp ground cinnamon

1 tsp ground cumin

1 tsp turmeric

1 tsp ground ginger

pinch of cayenne pepper

1/2 tsp red food coloring

3 to 3 1/2 lb chicken parts

1 Place yogurt in a mixing bowl large enough to hold chicken. Mix in lime juice, garlic, coriander, cinnamon, cumin, turmeric, ginger, pepper, and red food coloring. Stir to combine well.

2 Using a fork, pierce skin of chicken with a fork several times so that marinade can penetrate. Place chicken in bowl, and coat each part of chicken with yogurt mixture. Cover bowl with plastic wrap and refrigerate 24 hours. Do not cheat on marinating time, because the chicken needs this long to absorb flavors.

3 Just before you are ready to grill the chicken, remove it from bowl and arrange in a 2-qt rectangular glass dish. Place the meaty parts toward the outside of the dish. Cover with waxed paper. **MW on high** for 10 minutes.

4 Grill chicken over medium-hot coals until brown, basting with marinade occasionally. Keep grill covered for maximum smoky flavor.

Serving Suggestion
Kabuli Rice (page 155) from Afghanistan is a natural side dish for this Indian poultry dish. For a salad, serve sliced ripe avocados and grapefruit sections with a poppyseed dressing. As a beverage, choose a chilled semi-sweet white wine.

NOTE
Authentic Indian Tandoori Murg is baked in a tandoor. This clay pot is shaped like the huge jar in which Ali Baba hid from the Forty Thieves. The tandoor is usually sunk into the ground. A charcoal fire is built in the bottom of the jar about 2 hours before the food is to be put in, so that the sides of the jar will become scorching hot.

The chicken is marinated in the yogurt "masala," then roasted over the coals in the hot tandoor. The food takes on a characteristic flavor and red color. You can achieve a similar effect by grilling the marinated chicken outdoors.

Tangy Lemon Chicken

0.40* ✳ 547 cals

*plus marinating time

Serves 4

7 Tbsp olive oil
3 Tbsp red wine vinegar
1 tsp dried oregano leaves
¹/₄ tsp coarsely ground black pepper
1 cut-up chicken or chicken parts, 2¹/₂ to 3 lb
¹/₃ cup fresh lemon juice
1 large clove garlic, finely minced
4 Tbsp chopped fresh parsley

1 In a mixing bowl large enough to hold the chicken, mix 3 Tbsp olive oil, vinegar, oregano, and pepper. Place chicken in bowl and turn each piece to coat with mixture. Let stand 30 minutes.

2 In a 1-cup glass measure, combine lemon juice, remaining olive oil, garlic, and parsley; set aside. Use as a sauce for basting chicken on grill.

3 Arrange chicken pieces in a single layer in a 2-qt rectangular dish. Place thick pieces near the outside of the dish, and thin or bony pieces in the center. Cover with waxed paper. Turning each piece over midway through cooking, **MW on high** for 5 minutes per pound. Pour off drippings and discard.

4 Grill chicken over a medium fire for about 15 to 20 minutes, basting often with lemon juice mixture and turning as needed. Keep grill covered for maximum smoky flavor.

Serving Suggestion

This simple entree can go with a side dish containing a combination of foods. Easy Eggplant Parmigiana (page 152) would add a European flavor. Serve with a chilled German white wine.

OLIVE OIL

According to connoisseurs, Italian olive oil from Lucca, Tuscany, is the best in the world. The oil is pressed from tree-ripened olives; oil from the first pressing is termed "extra virgin" and is the finest. The best olive oil is clear and golden. Green-colored oils are fruitier and cloudy ones are inferior.

Most good olive oils will maintain their freshness indefinitely if kept in a tightly sealed bottle or can, in a relatively cool, dry place away from direct light. In very hot, humid climates, olive oil may need to be kept in the refrigerator, which will make it cloudy but has little effect on flavor.

Olive oil contains no cholesterol and is very digestible. Tests conducted by the American Heart Association's Nutrition Committee proved that using olive oil in place of saturated fats in the diet reduces blood cholesterol levels.

Low heat should be used when cooking with olive oil because it smokes at a lower temperature than other edible oils. It should not be used for deep-fat frying.

HOT & SPICY BARBECUED SPARERIBS

| 0.35* | 🍴 | $$ | 778 cals |

*plus marinating time

Serves 4

3 to 3½ lb country-style spareribs

1 cup water

4 Tbsp margarine or butter

1 cup ketchup

½ cup red wine vinegar

2 Tbsp Worcestershire sauce

1 Tbsp brown sugar

1 Tbsp instant minced onion

2 tsp dry mustard

1 tsp Liquid Smoke

½ to 1 tsp cayenne pepper

¼ tsp garlic powder

¼ tsp Tabasco sauce

1 Arrange spareribs in a single layer in a 2-qt rectangular dish. Pour water over spareribs and cover with waxed paper. **MW on high** for 8 minutes.

2 Turn each rib over and exchange ribs in the center of the dish for ribs at the outer edges. Re-cover dish and **MW on high** for 7 minutes. Pour off water and accumulated juices. Set ribs aside.

3 To make barbecue sauce, place margarine in a 4-cup glass measure. **MW on high** for 40 to 60 seconds, or until melted.

4 Add ketchup, vinegar, Worcestershire sauce, brown sugar, onion, mustard, Liquid Smoke, cayenne pepper, garlic powder, and Tabasco. **MW on high** until mixture begins to boil.

5 Grill ribs over a medium fire for 20 to 30 minutes, basting often with barbecue sauce and turning as needed. Keep grill covered for maximum smoky flavor. Serve with additional barbecue sauce. Pour remaining sauce into a jar and refrigerate for later use.

NOTE

Recipe makes 2 cups sauce. This barbecue sauce is also good on chicken.

Serving Suggestion

A great vegetable on the grill or in the microwave, Corn on the Cob, Olé (page 151) is a natural accompaniment. Serve with cold beer. To cool the palate from this spicy barbecued dinner, have a Banana Cream Pie (page 156) for dessert.

VINEGAR — THE ACID TEST

Although considered a staple item to be stored on a pantry shelf, vinegar can spoil. Maximum storage time for cider and distilled vinegars is about 6 months. Since wine and herbal vinegars are less acid, they will last at room temperature only about 2 to 3 months. We recommend storing wine vinegars in the refrigerator to retain optimum quality.

Vinegars should be stored in their own bottles, tightly capped, on a cool, dark, dry shelf. An unopened bottle will last almost indefinitely, but once opened, it is exposed to airborne yeasts and molds. Vinegar may cloud, mold, leave a sediment in the bottom, or grow a jellylike layer on top known as a "mother." The mother is harmless and can be removed by pouring the vinegar through a paper towel-lined tea strainer into a clean jar.

Once a vinegar clouds or shows sediment, use it promptly. Discard it if badly clouded.

GYROS *(Spitted spiced lamb)*

0.20*	✳	532 cals

*plus marinating time

Serves 4

1 slice bread

1 tsp salt

¹/₂ tsp coarsely ground black pepper

¹/₂ tsp ground allspice

³/₄ tsp ground coriander

1 Tbsp chopped fresh parsley

¹/₂ cup finely chopped onion

1 clove garlic, minced

1 lb ground lamb

2 slices bacon

1 tomato, chopped

1 Tbsp olive oil

1 Tbsp wine vinegar

shredded lettuce

6 oz plain yogurt

2 Tbsp chopped fresh parsley or dill

2 to 4 pita breads

1 Tear bread slice into chunks and put in blender or food processor. Pulse to make soft crumbs.

2 Place crumbs in a mixing bowl with salt, pepper, allspice, and ¹/₂ tsp coriander. Toss to distribute spices evenly. Add parsley, onion, garlic, and lamb. Combine well.

3 Make 16 meatballs from mixture, and flatten slightly to a thickness of ³/₄ in.

4 Place bacon on a folded paper towel. Lay across a plate and cover with another paper towel. **MW on high** for 1¹/₂ minutes. Bacon should not be completely done. Cut each slice into 8 pieces.

5 Grease four 10-in bamboo skewers. On each skewer, alternate meatballs and bacon pieces. Refrigerate 2 hours or overnight so that flavors blend and meatballs solidify on skewers.

6 Grill gyros outdoors to desired doneness or microwave. To microwave, place skewers on a meat or bacon rack and cover with waxed paper. Exchanging position of skewers on rack midway through cooking. **MW on 70% (medium-high)** for 6 to 8 minutes.

7 In one bowl, combine tomato, olive oil, vinegar, and ¹/₄ tsp coriander. Place lettuce in a second bowl. In a third bowl, combine yogurt and parsley. If heated pita bread is desired, wrap in paper towels and **MW on high** for 15 seconds per bread. Cut breads in half and open "pockets." Place all ingredients on table and let each person assemble his own gyro.

Serving Suggestion
A nice accompaniment would be Greek Green Beans (page 149) and a Greek wine such as Domestica.

NOTE
"Gyro, gyro oli" is a favorite children's game in Greece, comparable to "Farmer in the Dell," which describes the round-and-round motion of "gyro." Gyros have spread to Greece from the Middle East, and now have arrived in the United States. The meat is traditionally roasted to spicy crispness on a vertical spit, which turns electrically or manually by the mikro (apprentice). This recipe is a microwave version of the tasty snack from Crete.

LIME-MARINATED LAMB CHOPS

0.30*	✳	709 cals

*plus marinating time

Serves 2

2 limes

2 Tbsp tarragon or wine vinegar

¼ tsp ground rosemary

4 shoulder arm or shoulder blade lamb chops, about 1½ lb

seasoned salt

1 Grate the zest from the limes into a 8-in square glass dish. Squeeze juice from limes into dish, then add vinegar and rosemary; mix.

2 Sprinkle both sides of lamb chops with seasoned salt and pierce with a fork at 1-in intervals. Place lamb chops in marinade and turn to coat both sides. Cover dish and refrigerate at least 4 hours, or as long as 24 hours, turning chops over once.

3 Just before you are ready to grill the chops, turn them again in marinade so that both sides are coated well. Arrange in same dish with meat toward the outside and bones in the center. Cover with waxed paper. **MW on 50% (medium)** for 5 to 6 minutes, rotating plate midway through cooking.

4 Grill chops over medium-hot coals to desired doneness, basting with marinade occasionally.

Serving Suggestion

Much of the lamb we see in the supermarkets comes from New Zealand. Add a Pacific Island recipe of Tahitian Green Beans (page 150) for a nice accompaniment, along with a tropical fruit salad. Serve with a chilled rosé wine.

ZEST

The zest is the outer coating of citrus fruits such as lemons or limes. To obtain the zest, scrape the fruit against the medium side of a grater. Grate only the color off the fruit and do not grate too deeply, because the white part of the rind is very bitter.

Sometimes the term "grated peel" is used instead of zest. If you use a vegetable peeler to pare a long, thin strip of zest, this is known as "a twist," and is used for drinks "with a twist..." (of lemon, for example).

LAMB

Approximately 300 million pounds of lamb are produced in the United States yearly, and around 40 million pounds more are imported from Australia and New Zealand. Besides being a delicious change from other red meats, lamb is more healthful for you. Only 6 g of fat are contained in a 3-oz serving.

Lamb is meat from sheep less than one year old. Because it is young, it is very tender. Even though it is

available all year, meat labelled "Spring lamb" has been slaughtered between March and September. The color of lamb varies with the age of the animal. Light pink meat is from young, milk-fed lambs while the pinkish red meat comes from older animals.

As in microwaving other meats, the most tender cuts can be cooked on the faster power levels. Less tender cuts such as roasts and whole legs should be microwaved more slowly on a lower power level.

Top o' the Morning

Whether it's a leisurely weekend brunch or a quick hot breakfast before leaving for work, the microwave is tops for the morning. We've included some favorite breakfasts and brunches here, plus given directions for microwaving all types of eggs, breakfast meats, and hot cereals. Microwaving a mug of water for tea or coffee is up to you!

EGGS CREOLE

| 1.00 | 🍴 🍴 ✳ * | 1000 cals |

*freeze sauce and grits separately

Serves 4

4 servings hominy grits

2 Tbsp unsalted butter

1 cup finely chopped andouille or other fully-cooked spicy sausage

4 Tbsp shredded Cheddar cheese

1 large egg beaten with 1 Tbsp milk

seasoned dry bread crumbs

4 Tbsp oil

8 poached eggs

4 slices cooked breakfast sausage

1 A day in advance, prepare 4 servings of hominy grits according to package directions, or see microwave directions on page 140. When cooked, stir in butter, sausage, and cheese. Chill until firm enough to handle.

2 Make 8 balls of the grits mixture and flatten them like hamburger patties to a ½-in thickness. Place between squares of waxed paper so they won't stick together. Chill 24 hours.

3 Dust each grits patty with flour. Beat egg and milk together in a pie plate. Dip floured patties into egg and milk mixture, and coat with bread crumbs. Heat oil in a skillet on the stove. Fry the grits patties on both sides and keep warm.

4 Put 2 fried grits patties on each of 4 dinner plates. Top each patty with a poached egg and ladle Creole Sauce over all. Arrange a sausage slice on each plate. Serve immediately.

CREOLE SAUCE

1 cup julienned onion

1 cup julienned green pepper

2 ribs celery, julienned

2 cloves garlic, thinly sliced

1 bay leaf

2 Tbsp margarine or butter

1 can (16-oz) tomatoes

1 cup tomato juice

4 tsp Worcestershire sauce

4 tsp Louisiana Red Hot Sauce

2 tsp paprika

1½ Tbsp cornstarch

1 Place onion, bell pepper, and celery strips, garlic, bay leaf, and margarine in a 2-qt glass batter bowl. Cover with plastic wrap. **MW on high** for 5 minutes.

2 Pour liquid from canned tomatoes into a small mixing bowl; set aside. Coarsely chop tomatoes and add to vegetables in bowl. Add tomato juice, Worcestershire, hot sauce, and paprika. Stir well. Re-cover and **MW on high** for 5 minutes.

3 Using a wire whisk, blend cornstarch into reserved tomato liquid. Stir cornstarch mixture into heated sauce in bowl. Re-cover and **MW on high** for 5 to 6 minutes, or until sauce is bubbly hot and thickened. Makes 2 cups.

EGGS BENEDICT

| 0.20 | 🍳 | 573*cals |

*without gin fizz

Serves 2

Microwave Hollandaise Sauce

4 large eggs

2 English muffins

4 slices Canadian bacon

butter

1 Make Hollandaise sauce and set aside.

2 Poach eggs according to directions on page 140. While eggs are microwaving, use a fork to split muffins; toast conventionally.

3 Separate bacon and put slices on a dinner plate. After eggs come out of the microwave oven, put plate of bacon in oven. **MW on high** for 1 to 1½ minutes, or until hot.

4 To assemble Eggs Benedict, lightly butter the toasted English muffin halves. Put two halves on each dinner plate. Top each muffin half with a slice of hot Canadian bacon. Put an egg on top of each. Pour some of the Hollandaise sauce over. Serve immediately.

NOTE
Use the 2 egg whites left over from the Hollandaise sauce to make Ramos Gin Fizz, a popular New Orleans brunch drink.

MICROWAVE HOLLANDAISE SAUCE

½ cup butter or margarine

2 large eggs

2 Tbsp fresh lemon juice

1 Tbsp vermouth or dry white wine

½ tsp Worcestershire sauce

cayenne pepper

salt to taste

1 Place butter in a 2-cup glass measure. Cover with plastic wrap and **MW on high** for 1½ minutes, or until boiling.

2 Separate yolks from whites of eggs according to directions on page 103. Put yolks into a blender or food processor. Set whites aside for another use. Add lemon juice, vermouth, and Worcestershire sauce to yolks in blender, and blend well. Sprinkle a little cayenne pepper on the surface of the mixture.

3 When butter is bubbling, turn blender on and remove feeder cap from blender lid. Pour hot butter in a steady stream through the opening in lid. Blend about 30 seconds. Transfer mixture to same cup used to melt butter.

4 Just before pouring sauce over eggs or vegetables, **MW on 50% (medium)** for 30 to 60 seconds, stirring with a small whisk after every 15 seconds. Sauce should thicken slightly and be warm. Makes 1¼ cups.

NOTE
Since egg yolks are the only thickening ingredient in Hollandaise sauce, be very careful when reheating the sauce. If you microwave it too long, you will end up with scrambled eggs instead of a smooth, elegant sauce.

You will probably need only half this sauce for the Eggs Benedict recipe. Refrigerate leftover sauce in a glass jar. It will keep up to a week. To warm refrigerated sauce, remove lid and set jar on counter to come to room temperature. Then **MW on 50% (medium)** for 15 seconds. Stir with a small wire whisk. Repeat procedure until sauce is warm.

Hollandaise sauce is also delicious served over cooked green vegetables, such as asparagus, broccoli or Brussels sprouts, or on fish or veal.

RAMOS GIN FIZZ

Serves 2

4 Tbsp heavy cream

4 Tbsp milk

3 oz gin

2 large egg whites

2 Tbsp fresh lemon juice

1 Tbsp sugar

1 tsp orange flower water

2 cups crushed ice

In an electric blender, combine cream, milk, gin, egg whites, lemon juice, sugar, and orange flower water. Add ice and blend on high speed for 5 to 10 seconds or until thick and airy. Pour into two 9-oz old-fashioned glasses.

NOTE
These drinks may also be made in a cocktail shaker. Shake several minutes, or until frothy. Strain into glasses.

BREAKFAST MEATS IN THE MICROWAVE

Bacon People use their microwave ovens for heating a mug of water to make instant coffee or tea, baking potatoes, and reheating leftovers. But the food microwaved most often is bacon. The microwave does a wonderful job of cooking the fat out of bacon, leaving crisp and straight strips.

To microwave 1 to 4 slices of bacon, put paper towels on a microwave-safe dinner plate or paper plate. Cover with a paper towel. **MW on high** for 45 to 60 seconds per slice, turning the plate halfway around midway through cooking. The paper towels absorb grease, which cooks out of the bacon. Remove bacon from paper towels. Bacon will become more crisp as it stands.

Five or more slices of bacon create too much grease for one plate to contain, and so this much bacon should be microwaved on a bacon rack. To make the bacon rack easier to clean, put one paper towel on the rack. Then make one layer of bacon slices on top of the paper towel. If you want to cook more than one layer of bacon, put another paper towel on top of the bacon, and lay more slices in a crosswise direction on top of the first layer. Put a final paper towel over top layer of bacon to prevent spatters in the oven. **MW on high** for 30 to 45 seconds per slice, turning the rack halfway around midway through cooking. Look at the cooked bacon, and add more time if you think it will not become as crisp as you like it after standing.

Canadian Bacon Separate the slices of Canadian bacon and arrange in a circle on a microwave-safe plate. **MW on high** for 15 to 20 seconds per slice.

Sausage Patties and uncooked link sausage look unattractive when microwaved. Even if cooked on a microwave browning grill, they do not acquire the beautiful crisp, brown exterior that comes from conventional cooking in a skillet or broiler.

Fully cooked links and already-browned sausages microwave well. Be sure to pierce any casing with a fork for the steam to vent. Place on a paper towel to absorb grease. **MW on high** for 3 to 4 minutes per pound.

HOT NEWS!

The microwave oven uses less electricity than other cooking appliances. However, the money you save on your electric bill can easily be spent on paper towels. A woman once told us that she had a solution to the problem of so many paper towels; she put a section of the newspaper on the floor of her microwave oven and on top of that, she put one paper towel and her bacon slices.

Don't ever put newspapers in the microwave oven! The lead in the ink combined with newsprint paper can start a fire. Hot bacon grease makes the chances for a fire even greater. Keep "hot news" out of your oven!

SICILIAN FRITTATA

| 0.22 | ✳ | 173 cals |

Serves 6

1 package (10-oz) frozen chopped broccoli
6 large eggs
1/2 cup milk
1/2 tsp dried oregano
1/2 tsp dried basil
1/2 tsp salt
1/4 tsp garlic powder
1/8 tsp white pepper
1 cup grated mozzarella cheese
1 can (2 1/4-oz) sliced black olives, drained
2 tsp grated Parmesan cheese

1 If broccoli is wrapped in foil packaging, remove wrapper. If wrapper is waxed paper, do not remove. Place package of broccoli on a paper towel. **MW on high** for 5 to 6 minutes. Drain liquid thoroughly from box; set aside.

2 In a mixing bowl, beat together eggs, milk, oregano, basil, salt, garlic powder, and white pepper. Stir in cooked broccoli, mozzarella cheese, and half the olives.

3 Spray an 8-in round glass dish with a vegetable coating (such as Pam). Pour egg mixture into dish. Top with remaining olives and sprinkle with Parmesan cheese. Rotating ¼ turn every 3 minutes, **MW on 70% (medium-high)** for 12 minutes, or until set. Let stand 10 minutes before cutting.

NOTE
Frittatas are similar to quiches without crusts. They contain more eggs than quiches, but the fillings can be just as varied.

Because of the large number of eggs in a frittata, we do not recommend microwaving on high power. Instead, use 70% or 50% power. An 8-in round glass cake dish is a perfect utensil.

SEPARATING EGGS
Be careful when separating eggs because as much as just a speck of egg yolk in the whites makes it impossible to beat them.

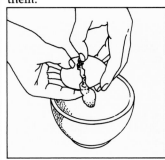

Give egg a sharp rap on the side of bowl. Gently pull shell apart with your thumbs.

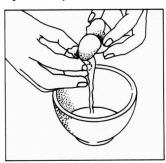

Transfer yolk from one shell half to other until white runs out of shell. Put yolk in another bowl.

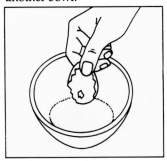

If a small piece of shell or a speck of egg yolk has fallen into the white, scoop it out using one of the empty half-shells.

HUEVOS REVUELTOS DE RANCHO

| 0.40 | 169 cals |

Serves 2

2 eggs

2 Tbsp salsa of your choice

2 corn tortillas, heated

2 Tbsp sour cream

2 tsp chopped fresh cilantro (Chinese parsley)

These are Mexican farmhouse scrambled eggs.

1 Beat eggs in a 1-in glass measure. **MW on high** for 40 seconds.

2 Beat eggs well, then stir in salsa. **MW on high** for 20 seconds, or until eggs are desired doneness.

3 Stir eggs and place half the mixture on each tortilla. Top each with 1 Tbsp of sour cream and sprinkle with cilantro. If desired, serve with additional salsa.

HEATING TORTILLAS

To keep flour or corn tortillas soft while heating, wrap 1 to 6 tortillas in a damp paper towel. Put the wrapped tortillas on a salad plate, and turn an identical size plate upside down over the tortillas. **MW on high** for 8 to 10 seconds per tortilla.

When tortillas are heated in this manner, they will be soft and moist. They can be rolled around ingredients for making enchiladas without breaking. Use heated tortillas for Farmhouse Scrambled Eggs, or other Mexican recipes. The heated tortillas can also be buttered and substitute for bread or rolls at meals.

LEEK TART

0.20 ☐ ☐ ✳ 421 cals

Serves 6

1 bunch leeks, about four 3/4-in

4 Tbsp margarine or butter

4 oz cooked ham, cubed

4 oz Swiss cheese

3 large eggs

3/4 cup half milk and heavy cream or all light cream

salt and black pepper to taste

9-in pie crust, baked

The following directions are for using a food processor to make this recipe. If you do not have one, use a chef's knife and cutting board to slice leeks and chop ham. Shred cheese using a grater. Assemble quiche as below.

1 Cut off green tops of leeks, leaving 2 in. Cut off roots and wash well to remove dirt trapped between layers. Pack into feed tube of a food processor and slice thinly, using light pressure through slicing disk. Transfer sliced leeks to a 4-cup glass measure. Add butter, cover with plastic wrap, and **MW on high** for 6 minutes.

2 Meanwhile, insert chopping blade in food processor. Add ham and pulse to chop finely. Remove blade and insert grater disk. Put cheese in feed tube and grate.

3 Add eggs and cream mixture to cooked leeks, then beat. Add ham, cheese, and salt and pepper to taste. Pour mixture into baked pie crust. Rotating dish a quarter turn every 3 minutes, **MW on 70% (medium-high)** for 9 to 10 minutes, or until center jiggles only slightly. Let stand 15 minutes before serving. Garnish with some of the tender green leek tops, if desired, but remove before eating.

MICROWAVING QUICHE

Quiche filling is a main-dish custard containing eggs, cheese, and cream. Because of the delicate cooking required of these ingredients, **MW on 70% (medium-high).** We also use this power level for reheating leftover quiche. The crust must be completely baked before filling.

Bake the crust in a heatproof glass pie dish. Always spray the pie dish with a nonstick vegetable spray before putting the raw crust into it so that the finished quiche will come out of the dish without sticking.

Prepare and roll out pastry. Spread crust evenly in the pan, bringing edges up and smoothing them against sides of pan. Trim excess, leaving about 1/2 extend over top. Flute edge.

Quiche is cooked when a knife inserted in center comes out clean. Let quiche stand for 10 minutes before serving.

HOT SAUSAGE QUICHE

| 0.16 | 🍳 | ✳ | 412 cals |

Serves 6

8 oz spicy bulk sausage

¹/₂ green bell pepper, chopped

¹/₄ cup chopped onion

³/₄ cup half and half or half milk and half heavy cream

3 large eggs

1¹/₂ cups grated sharp Cheddar cheese, about 6 oz

9-in pie crust, baked (see page 106)

paprika

1 Crumble sausage into a dishwasher-safe plastic colander set in a 1-qt casserole. Sprinkle bell pepper and onion over top. **MW on high** for 3¹/₂ to 4 minutes, stirring midway through cooking.

2 Drain and discard grease, and set aside sausage. Beat together cream mixture and eggs in same casserole. Stir in cheese and cooked sausage mixture.

3 Pour mixture into baked pie crust. Sprinkle with paprika. Rotating quiche every 3 minutes, **MW on 70% (medium-high)** for 9 to 10 minutes, or until center is set. Let stand at least 10 minutes before cutting.

CHEF'S CLASS
Bell Pepper Leftover

Many recipes use green or red bell peppers, but often you won't need an entire pepper. When you have part of a pepper left, there are two ways you can store it for future use.

Remove the seeds and membranes inside the pepper, and wash the pepper portion in cool water. Dry it with a paper towel and put it into a plastic sandwich bag or wrap it in plastic wrap. It will stay fresh 4 to 5 days in the refrigerator.

Prepare the pepper portion as above, but chop it before putting it into the plastic bag. Freeze the bag of chopped pepper. It can be stored in the freezer for up to 6 months. Once bell peppers have been frozen, they will not be crisp after defrosting, so only use in recipes in which pepper will be cooked.

Shredding Cheese

Semi-hard cheeses—such as Cheddar, Monterey Jack, or Mozzarella—should be chilled when you shred them. If you leave them out on the counter, they will soften and crumble when pushed against a hand grater or shredded in a food processor.

If you've got extra, put shredded cheese into small plastic bags, and label the bags with the name of the cheese, the weight, and the date. Keep refrigerated for up to 2 weeks. Shredded cheese can also be stored for up to 2 months in the freezer. To defrost frozen shredded cheese, transfer the bag to the refrigerator or let cheese stand at room temperature.

Directions for grating hard cheeses, such as Parmesan or Romano, can be found on page 25.

Sweet Endings

If your mother was like ours, dinner wasn't "dinner" without dessert. Of course a light dessert should follow a hearty meal. Too much richness and a diner usually feels overstuffed even before his dinner plate is removed, so he's certainly not going to take on a big piece of gooey cake or pie. But if you have served a light meal, that's the time to indulge in a sinfully rich dessert. The recipes here fall mostly into that latter category.

TEXAS CRUDE CAKE

| 0.30 | 🍴 ✳ | 740 cals |

Serves 8

1 cup margarine or butter

1/2 cup unsweetened cocoa

2 cups granulated sugar

4 large eggs

1 tsp baking powder

1/4 tsp salt

1 1/2 cups all-purpose flour

2 tsp vanilla extract

1/2 cup pecan pieces

1 1/4 cups miniature marshmallows

A one-layer chocolate cake as rich as the oil that made Texas millionaires!

1 Put margarine in a 2-qt batter bowl. **MW on high** for 1 1/2 to 2 minutes, or until melted.

2 Using a wooden spoon, beat in cocoa and sugar; then add eggs. Blend in baking powder, salt, and flour. Stir in vanilla and pecans.

3 Spread batter evenly in a 2-qt rectangular dish (8 x 12-in). Rotating dish a quarter turn every 3 minutes, **MW on 70% (medium-high)** for 11 to 12 minutes, or until cake tests done.

4 Leave cake in pan and distribute marshmallows evenly over hot cake. Cover with plastic wrap, and let stand 5 minutes. Uncover and spread melted marshmallows over top of cake; let cool.

CHOCOLATE FROSTING

2 Tbsp margarine or butter

2 Tbsp unsweetened cocoa

2 Tbsp milk

2 cups sifted confectioners sugar

1 tsp vanilla extract

1 Put margarine in a 4-cup glass measure. **MW on high** for 30 to 40 seconds, or until melted.

2 Stir in cocoa, then milk. Blend in sugar and vanilla to make a smooth frosting. Spread on top of cake in dish.

MICROWAVE CAKES

Always use a solid shortening (such as Crisco) to grease the pan. Do not dust with flour, however, because it will make the outside of the cake white. For layer cakes, cut waxed paper circles to fit the bottom of the pans. You may also need to shield a square or rectangular pan with aluminum foil, because the corners will cook twice as fast as the center. Use transparent or masking tape to affix 2 x 1-in rectangles of foil to the outside corners of the pan. In baking cake layers, bake only 1 layer at a time.

Don't blend microwave cake batters with an electric mixer. It beats too many air bubbles into the batter, which results in a coarse-textured product. Instead, sift the dry cake mix into the mixing bowl and use a wooden spoon to combine ingredients.

BILL STEINER'S LUSCIOUS LEMON CAKE

| 0.25 | ✳ | 563 cals |

Serves 10

¼ cup graham cracker crumbs

2-layer lemon cake mix, but not one with pudding

1 package (3⅝-oz) instant lemon pudding mix

1 cup water

½ cup oil

4 large eggs

½ cup margarine or butter

1 cup granulated sugar

1 Tbsp lemon extract

1 Using a solid shortening (such as Crisco), grease a 12-cup microwave Bundt pan. Sprinkle crumbs into pan and tilt to coat. Set aside.

2 So that the batter will not be lumpy, use a flour sifter to sift cake mix into a 2-qt mixing bowl. Add pudding mix, ¾ cup water, oil, and eggs. Use a wooden spoon to combine all ingredients. (Do not use an electric mixer, because it beats air bubbles into the batter.)

3 Pour batter into prepared pan and spread batter level. Rotating the pan a quarter turn every 3 minutes, **MW on 50% (medium)** for 8 minutes. Then **MW on high** for 4 to 4½ minutes. Cake is done when a toothpick inserted into it comes out clean. Cover cake with waxed paper, and let stand flat on counter.

4 Combine margarine, sugar, and remaining water in a 1-qt glass batter bowl. **MW on high** for 2 minutes, or until mixture begins to boil. Stir and **MW on high** for 1 minute after a boil is reached. Add lemon extract to mixture.

5 Use a long skewer or cake tester to poke holes at 1-in intervals through cake to the bottom of the pan. Pour lemon sauce evenly over cake. Let stand 5 minutes, or until all the sauce has been absorbed.

6 Shake pan gently to loosen cake, and invert onto a plate.

BUNDT PANS

A Bundt pan is not one of the basic cooking utensils we recommend buying (see page 133), but it can be used for other foods besides cakes. You can make a meatloaf in it, or a beautiful wreath of fresh vegetables. If you can find a clear plastic one, they're great for microwaving because you can see if the food is done at the bottom just by looking through it.

The Bundt pan came from Germany, and was originally used to make *kugelhof*, or coffee cakes. The pan was brought to America during the early 1900s, in the bottom of someone's steamer trunk. Nordic Ware started producing metal versions of the pan in 1950, and plastic pans are now manufactured for microwave use. The name "Bundt" is a registered trademark of Northland Aluminum Products, Inc.

JAMOCHA PECAN PIE

0.20	✳	636 cals

Serves 6

2 Tbsp water

2 Tbsp instant coffee powder

1 square (1-oz) unsweetened chocolate

2 Tbsp margarine or butter

3 large eggs

½ cup granulated sugar

1 cup light corn syrup

1¼ cups chopped pecans

9-in pie crust, baked

whipped topping or sweetened whipped cream

The flavors of coffee and chocolate make this pecan pie the richest of all!

1 Put water in a 1-qt glass batter bowl. **MW on high** for 45 to 50 seconds. Add the instant coffee to the water, and stir to dissolve.

2 Add chocolate and margarine to coffee mixture. **MW on high** for 1 minute, or until chocolate is melted. Add eggs, sugar, and corn syrup; beat well. Stir in pecans and pour into pie crust.

3 Rotating pie a half turn after 5 minutes of cooking, **MW on 50% (medium)** for 10 to 12 minutes. Pie is done when a knife inserted halfway between the outside and center comes out clean. Cool to lukewarm before cutting. Top each serving with whipped topping.

NOTE
We think that this pie tastes best when served warm. To warm a slice of pie, **MW on 70% (medium-high)** for 15 to 20 seconds.

PATABLE PIE CRUST

1¼ cups all-purpose flour

½ tsp salt

⅓ cup oil

2 Tbsp cold water

This is an easy, homemade pie crust that does not require cutting in the shortening or rolling out the dough. But, before you begin, read Do You Measure Up? (page 136) to ensure that your pie crust will be tender and flaky.

1 Put flour and salt in a medium mixing bowl. Using a fork, stir oil into dry ingredients until well combined. Sprinkle water over mixture and stir to make a dough.

2 Use Pam or an unfloured vegetable spray to coat a 9-in glass pie plate. Pick up dough and shape it into a ball. Flatten ball between your palms until it is about 1 in thick. Place it in the center of prepared pie plate. Using your fingers, pat dough in a uniform thickness onto bottom and up sides of pie plate.

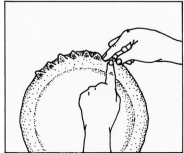

3 Around the top rim of plate, pinch pastry between your thumb and 2 index fingers to make a fluted edge.

4 Using same fork, prick bottom and sides of crust at 1-in intervals to prevent puffing during baking.

5 Rotating pie plate a quarter turn after 2 minutes of cooking, **MW on high** for 5 to 6 minutes, or until pie crust looks opaque and blistered.

NOTE

This recipe can also be baked in a conventional oven. Preheat to 450°F. Set pie plate on top shelf in oven. Bake 8 to 12 minutes, or until crust is golden brown.

DAVID CLIFFORD'S FRENCH COCONUT PIE

| 0.25 | ✳ | 368 cals |

Serves 8

5 Tbsp butter

1 cup granulated sugar

3 large eggs

1/2 cup buttermilk

1 tsp vanilla extract

1 can (3.5-oz) flaked coconut, about 1 1/3 cups

9-in pie shell, baked

1 Place 4 Tbsp butter in a 4-cup glass measure. **MW on high** for 1 minute, or until melted.

2 Beat in sugar, then eggs. Stir in buttermilk and vanilla. Reserve 1/3 cup coconut; set aside. Add remaining (1 cup) coconut to pie filling and pour into baked pie shell. Rotating dish every 3 minutes, **MW on 70% (medium-high)** for 9 to 10 minutes, or until center is set.

3 Toast reserved coconut. Place remaining Tbsp butter in a small casserole. **MW on high** until melted. Toss coconut with butter. Stirring every 30 seconds, **MW on high** for 3 minutes, or until coconut is toasted.

4 Sprinkle toasted coconut on top of pie. Serve.

FROZEN PIE CRUSTS

If pie is your idea of dessert, pre-bake the crust before adding a filling or use a commercial crust. Commercial frozen pie crusts are a time-saver for busy cooks, but they are frozen in aluminum foil pans. To use them in the microwave oven, transfer the frozen pie crust to a glass pie dish. Spray the glass pie dish with a vegetable coating such as Pam, so the baked pie will not stick to the dish.

To remove the frozen pie crust from the foil pan, bend the aluminum rim down, away from the pastry. Continue bending it all around, and the pie crust will pop right out. Don't let the crust defrost before trying to remove it, because it will tear into strips!

Place the frozen pie crust in your prepared pie dish, and let it defrost at room temperature a few minutes. When you can mold the pastry without cracking it, flute the edge to fit the dish, and prick with a fork all over. If more browning is desired, brush rim with vanilla. Turning dish halfway around after 2 minutes, **MW on high** for 4 to 5 minutes, or until pastry looks blistered and flaky. Pour filling into crust and bake again. The second time around, only the filling will cook.

CHERRY ALMOND PIE

| 0.12 | ✳ | 497 cals |

Serves 6

1 Tbsp Amaretto liqueur

1 jar (25-oz) cherry pie filling (see note)

9-in pie crust, baked

¹⁄₃ cup all-purpose flour

4 Tbsp margarine or butter

4 Tbsp packed brown sugar

¹⁄₂ cup uncooked quick oats

¹⁄₃ cup sliced almonds

1 Stir liqueur into pie filling and pour into baked pie crust.

2 If you have a food processor, put steel blade in processor bowl and add flour. Cut margarine into chunks, and add to flour. Pulse on and off until margarine is in tiny chunks. Add brown sugar; pulse briefly. Add oats; pulse briefly again. If you don't have a food processor, place flour and margarine in a mixing bowl, then use a pastry blender or 2 knives to cut margarine into flour. Stir in brown sugar and oats.

3 Distribute this crumb mixture over the top of pie. Scatter almonds on top. **MW on high** for 5 to 6 minutes, or until heated throughout. Let cool before slicing.

NOTE
An Apple Rum Pie can also be made from this recipe. Substitute rum for the liqueur, and apple pie filling for the cherry. Add 1 tsp of ground cinnamon to the filling.

The flavors of cherries and almonds are very compatible. In fact, during the process of making maraschino cherries, the fruits are steeped in almond flavoring to give them their characteristic flavor.

Amaretto liqueur has an almond flavor, but it is not made from almonds. This liqueur is distilled from apricot pits. The apricot family, however, is related to the almond family.

SOFTENING BROWN SUGAR
Once a box of brown sugar has been opened, the sugar will begin to dry out and harden. One way to store brown sugar is to empty it into a zip-locking plastic bag, then seal out as much air as possible. Put the plastic bag of sugar into a glass jar with a screw lid.

Despite your best efforts, the brown sugar may get hard after a few weeks. Use the microwave oven to soften the brown sugar so that it is usable again. Put a piece of bread or a slice of apple into the container of brown sugar, and **MW on high** for 15 to 30 seconds. The moisture from the bread or apple will put moisture back into the sugar.

MANDARIN CHEESE PIE

| 0.20 | ✳ | 457 cals |

Serves 8

4 Tbsp margarine or butter

1¼ cups graham cracker crumbs

¾ cup granulated sugar

1 package (8-oz) cream cheese

1 tsp lemon juice

2 Tbsp Triple Sec or Cointreau liqueur

1 tsp grated orange peel

2 large eggs

2 cups sour cream

1 can (10-oz) mandarin oranges

This cheesecake is made in a pie plate. The hint of orange flavor comes from the liqueur, and makes it a soothing but rich dessert.

1 Put margarine in a 9-in glass pie plate. **MW on high** for 40 seconds, or until melted.

2 Add crumbs and 2 Tbsp sugar to margarine in plate. Stir mixture until combined well. Use the back of a spoon to press mixture uniformly onto bottom and up sides of pie plate. **MW on high** for 2 minutes, rotating pie plate a half turn after 1 minute of cooking. Set aside.

3 Unwrap cream cheese and place in small glass bowl of electric mixer. **MW on 50% (medium)** for 1½ minutes, or until softened. Turn mixer on medium speed and beat cheese 15 seconds. Leave mixer on and add ½ cup sugar. Beat until well combined. Add lemon juice, 1 Tbsp liqueur, and orange peel.

4 Crack eggs into mixture and beat about 30 seconds. Pour filling into baked crust. **MW on 70% (medium-high)** for 6 to 7 minutes, rotating pie plate a quarter turn every 2 minutes.

5 While cheesecake is baking, assemble topping by mixing together sour cream and remaining 2 Tbsp sugar. Add 1 Tbsp liqueur. Spread on top of baked cheesecake. **MW on 70%** for 2 to 3 minutes. Let cool to lukewarm; then, refrigerate.

6 Just before serving, drain liquid from can or oranges. Decorate cheesecake by making a row of orange slices around the top.

SOFTENING CREAM CHEESE

To soften cream cheese for spreading or combining with other ingredients, put the unwrapped package(s) into a glass bowl or dish. **MW on 50% (medium)** so that the cream cheese will become soft. (Do not use high power because it will melt, and possibly curdle.) For a 3-oz package, microwave for 45 to 60 seconds; for an 8-oz package, microwave for 1 to 1½ minutes.

CHOCOLATE FUDGE SHEBA

| 0.15* | $$ | 414 cals |

*plus chilling time

Serves 6

½ cup chopped pecans

1 package (8-oz) semi-sweet chocolate

5 Tbsp butter

3 large eggs

¼ cup granulated sugar

whipped topping or sweetened whipped cream

This is the most popular dessert on the menu at Commander's Palace in New Orleans.

1 Tear off a 12-in piece from a roll of plastic wrap. Place in bottom of a 9 x 5 x 3-in loaf pan, so that the ends of the plastic wrap are draped over the sides of the pan. Sprinkle half the pecans evenly in bottom of lined pan. Set remaining pecans aside.

2 Unwrap squares of chocolate. Place chocolate and butter in a 2-qt glass batter bowl. **MW on high** for 3 to 3½ minutes, or until chocolate melts. Using a wire whisk, stir well.

3 Separate yolk from white of each egg (see page 103). Put whites in the small bowl of an electric mixer; set aside. Using a fork, beat yolks in a small bowl. Add yolks to melted chocolate, and stir with whisk until mixture thickens slightly and cools to lukewarm.

4 Beat egg whites on highest speed of electric mixer until they form soft peaks. Turn mixer on again and add sugar gradually. Beat until mixture holds stiff peaks. Using a rubber spatula, scrape beaten egg whites from bowl and pile on top of chocolate mixture. Fold chocolate mixture into egg whites until the mixture is one color throughout.

5 Scrape mixture into prepared pan and sprinkle remaining pecans over top. Refrigerate at least 2 hours, or until firm. To serve, lift dessert out of dish by pulling on ends of plastic wrap. Slice and put on dessert plates. Top each serving with whipped topping or sweetened whipped cream.

FOLDING

The best utensil for folding egg whites or whipped cream is a rubber spatula. Cut down through the center to the bottom of the bowl, scraping heavier mixture up from bot-

tom of bowl through lighter mixture.
Give bowl a quarter turn, and lightly repeat until mixtures are combined.

CHOCOLATE MOCHA MOUSSE

| 0.10* | $$ | 387 cals |

*plus chilling time

Serves 6

6 squares (1-oz) semi-sweet chocolate

¼ cup water

1 tsp instant coffee powder

2 large eggs

½ cup granulated sugar

2 Tbsp coffee liqueur, such as Kahlua

1 cup heavy cream

1 Combine chocolate, water, and coffee powder in a 2-qt glass bowl. **MW on 50% (medium)** for 2½ to 3 minutes, or until chocolate is melted.

2 Mix in eggs, until mixture thickens slightly. Stir in sugar and coffee liqueur. Let cool to room temperature.

3 Beat cream until it holds a soft shape and is still glossy. (Do not overbeat or it will turn into butter!) Fold (see page 122) whipped cream into chocolate mixture.

4 Spoon into six 4-oz sherbet or champagne glasses. Refrigerate 2 hours or more before serving. Garnish with a rosette of whipped cream dusted lightly with cocoa.

MELTING CHOCOLATE

To melt chocolate on a conventional stove, you must use a double boiler. The chocolate can scorch, due to the high cocoa butter content, therefore, the chocolate has to be melted over hot water, with indirect heat.

Melting chocolate is much easier, however, in a microwave. Put the unwrapped chocolate in a glass bowl and **MW on 50% (medium)** according to the following times: For 1 oz (1 square) of semi-sweet or unsweetened chocolate, microwave 1 to 2 minutes.

For chocolate chips, microwave 2½ to 3 minutes for 6 oz (1 cup) and 5 to 6 minutes for 12 oz (2 cups). If you are melting the chocolate along with margarine or other ingredients, you can use a higher power level.

Stir the chocolate midway through the melting time. In the microwave oven, chocolate will become soft while maintaining its original shape. You may look through the oven window and think that the chocolate is still solid, but it may be softer than you think. But beware! If you microwave chocolate too long, it can scorch or burn just as it can on a conventional stove.

BILL RODGERS' BLUEBERRY CRISP

| 0.10 | ✳ | 152 cals |

Serves 6

½ cup granulated sugar

⅓ cup all-purpose flour

1 tsp ground cinnamon

¼ tsp ground ginger

2 Tbsp margarine or butter

2 cups fresh blueberries, washed and drained

1 Tbsp fresh lemon juice

vanilla ice cream

World-renowned marathon runner Bill Rodgers shares a favorite recipe with us. Bill and his wife pick bushels of wild blueberries on their land. As Bill says, "This is a great dessert and so easy even I can make it!"

1 In a small bowl, combine sugar, flour, cinnamon, and ginger. Place margarine in a 9-in glass pie plate, and **MW on high** for 30 seconds, or until melted.

2 Add melted margarine to dry ingredients; blend thoroughly. Set aside.

3 Place blueberries in same 9-in glass pie plate. Sprinkle lemon juice over top. Distribute reserved crumb mixture over top of blueberries. **MW on high** for to 5 minutes, rotating dish midway through cooking.

4 Let dessert stand a few minutes for the topping to become more crisp. Spoon dessert over scoops of vanilla ice cream.

BLUEBERRIES

If you found your thrill on blueberry hill, you might like to know a little more about this fruit. Cultivated high-bush blueberries grow on bushes from 1 to 20 feet high in most places on the North American continent. Wild low-bush blueberries grow low to the ground, in cold, wet "barrens" or bogs, such as in Maine. Blueberries are an old Indian food which supplied many tribes who ate them fresh, cooked, or dried.

The peak season for fresh blueberries is June, July, and August. They are also available canned and frozen all year long. Sometimes blueberries are called huckleberries, but there are some differences. Blueberries are lighter in color and have very tiny—almost unnoticeable—seeds. Huckleberries are almost black in color with hard seedlike nutlets. Huckleberries are always found wild, but blueberries are cultivated for commercial crops.

When choosing blueberries at the store, select clean, plump berries with a deep blue color. They may be covered with a light-colored bloom. Store them in the refrigerator, and use them within 2 or 3 days. You can also freeze them in plastic bags after washing and draining them well.

GEORGE BUSH'S PRALINES

0.15	110 cals*

*each

Makes 24 pralines

1 lb light brown sugar

1 can (5⅓ oz) evaporated milk

1 cup pecan halves

1 Cover 2 cookie sheets with waxed paper. Set aside.

2 Use a wooden spoon to mix brown sugar and milk in a 2-qt glass batter bowl. Stir well to make sure there are no lumps, which tend to burn during microwaving.

3 Add pecans. **MW on high** for 6 minutes. Stir, then **MW on high** for 3 minutes, or until mixture reaches 248°F. on a candy thermometer, the soft-ball stage.

4 Use the wooden spoon to beat the mixture about 3 minutes, or until it begins to thicken. Drop by tablespoonfuls onto waxed paper. Let harden completely before pulling off paper. Store pralines in an air-tight container.

HOW SWEET IT IS!

Never consider making candy without several sizes of heat-resistant glass measuring cups. The best type is the glass "batter bowl." Available in 1- and 2-qt sizes, these large, bowl-shaped measurers have a pouring spout and a handle which always stays cool.

If you are making a recipe that is microwaved to 248°F., use a microwave candy thermometer. Do not use a conventional candy thermometer in the microwave because the mercury and metal parts are not microwave safe.

USEFUL INFORMATION AND BASIC RECIPES

Micro Kitchen Information

Microwave cooking is easy if you understand a few basic principles. We describe here how the oven works, which power levels to use, how the microwaves affect food, which way to arrange the food for optimum cooking results, and how many minutes foods should be cooked. We've also given you some other basic tips, such as guidelines for equipping a kitchen and a substitution chart to use when you don't have a needed ingredient.

Microwave Ovenworks

What's behind it all? The microwave controls, that is. If you learn how the oven works, you can microwave food better, and avoid unnecessary repairs.

Let's plug it in. One of the causes of oven damage is doing it wrong. The microwave oven plug has 3 prongs for a good reason: The round prong provides a ground for the appliance which is independent of the household power lines. This protects you from an electric shock caused by accidental grounding.

Never detach the round prong from the microwave oven plug to fit it into a 2-prong outlet. If your kitchen does not have a 3-prong outlet, buy an adaptor plug and ground it by attaching the short wire to the screw on the plastic or metal cover plate of the outlet.

The wall outlet should be a dedicated or isolated circuit, which means that the only thing operating on it is the microwave oven. The usual household circuit is 15 amps, and a microwave oven uses about 13.5 amps. If other appliances are plugged in to the same circuit, the circuit may overload and blow fuses.

Another "no-no" is plugging the microwave oven into an extension cord. The National Electrical Code states that no appliance should be hooked to an extension cord. Power is lost over every foot of wire, and the output wattage drops around 10 watts for each one volt of drop; thus slower cooking results.

When the electricity enters the microwave oven, a low voltage transformer converts some of it to power the control panel. The oven's "brain" — a control board — is very expensive to repair. Keep the control panel clean.

The microwave oven will not operate until the safety interlock system is engaged. Depending on the brand, there are from 3 to 6 switches that keep the oven from running with the door open.

The main component of the microwave oven is the magnetron tube, which converts electricity into electromagnetic energy, or microwaves. Other components — such as transformers, rectifiers, and capacitors — convert the house current into a controlled voltage that activates the magnetron. According to several repairmen we talked to, only about 2 to 3% of their repairs are due to breakdown of the magnetron tube, which is a very expensive but dependable component. Fuses and switches go bad more than anything else.

According to microwave oven repair people, if you pop any type of popcorn in the microwave oven, or operate it empty, you may burn out 2 other oven components: the blower motor and the thermal protector. Popping popcorn is known as a "no-load" condition. There is practically no moisture in the corn to absorb the microwaves being emitted.

If you are having trouble with your microwave oven, read the operating manual and cookbook that came with it. Many repair calls are unnecessary and are due to customer ignorance.

"MAN" THE CONTROLS

The magnetron tube converts electricity into microwaves. They travel down a metal channel or "wave guide," and are dispersed into the oven cavity. One distribution system is a stir fan. Since metal reflects microwaves, rotating metal blades scatter the microwaves into the oven cavity to promote even cooking. Another system is the rotating turntable, which turns the food through a fixed field of microwave energy.

The oven interior is metal (either stainless or acrylic-coated steel), and this causes the microwaves to bounce off the walls until absorbed by food in the oven. The glass door is shielded with a perforated metal screen. The holes let you see what's cooking, but are not large enough to allow microwaves to escape into the room. Keep the door clean and free of grease buildup.

Because metal reflects microwave energy, don't use metal utensils in the microwave oven unless they were designed for microwave use. However, just as sunlight passes through a window, microwave energy passes through glass, paper, plastic, pyroceramic, wood, and straw, and these materials can be used for cooking. Microwave utensils can get hot to the touch because the heat from the food is transferred to the utensil, but the microwaves themselves do not make the utensil hot.

Microwaves penetrate the food 1 to 1½ in, and they activate the food molecules to vibrate. This vibration creates friction, which produces heat within the food itself. It is this heat that cooks the food. Because the food molecules are vibrating so rapidly, they do not stop immediately when the microwave oven turns off. That is why food continues to cook for about one-third of the time it was microwaved after oven shuts off.

When the microwave oven is on high power, the magnetron tube produces full-strength microwaves 100% of the time. Not all foods cook well on high power, and most microwave ovens today also have lower power levels which cook delicate foods slower and more gently.

The International Microwave Power Institute has established 5 universal power settings, which we have used for all the recipes in this book. They are:

100% —	**High**
70% —	**Medium-High**
50% —	**Medium**
30% —	**Medium-Low**
10% —	**Low**

The percentages are the proportion of time the magnetron is "on" (producing full strength microwaves). The remaining proportion of the time, the magnetron is "off" (producing no microwaves). For example, if you set the oven to cook for 20 minutes on 70% power, the magnetron tube will be producing full-strength microwaves 70% of the time (14 minutes), and it will be producing no microwaves 30% of the time (6 minutes). During the 20 minutes, the magnetron tube will cycle "on and off".

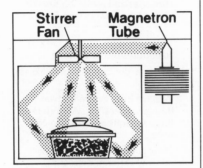

Stirrer Fan — **Magnetron Tube**

If your microwave oven has controls consisting of numbers 1 through 10, your power settings are easy to understand. Just add a zero to each number, and you will see the percentages of high power that these are. Use number 7 for 70% (medium-high), number 5 for 50% (medium)

If your microwave oven has controls displayed in words, look in your owner's manual to find the percentages of high power equivalent to the words. If you cannot find an explanation, send a self-addressed stamped envelope to: CiCi Williamson, "MicroScope," P. 0. Box 79762, Houston, TX 77279. Include the manufacturer's name, model number, year, and a list of the power settings printed on your control panel. An explanation will be sent to you.

ROGER STAUBACH'S SPINACH SALAD

Serves 4

1 bag (10 oz) fresh spinach
¾ cup sugar
1 tsp dry mustard
½ tsp salt
¼ tsp paprika
1 can (10¾-oz) condensed tomato soup
¾ cup oil
¾ cup vinegar
1 onion, quartered
4 oz Bleu cheese
1 can (2.8-oz) French-fried onion rings

There's no microwaving needed in this recipe, but we included it as a delicious accompaniment to entrees elsewhere in the book.

1 Fresh spinach leaves always have sand in them. Wash spinach in a sink full of warm water. The warm water sends the sand to the bottom. Repeat washing in cold running water. Remove stems and make layers of leaves on paper towels. Place in plastic bag to chill in refrigerator.

2 To make dressing for salad, mix sugar, dry mustard, salt, and paprika in a tall bottle. Add soup, oil, and vinegar; shake well. Put onion in for flavor, but remove before serving. Store dressing in refrigerator.

3. To assemble salad, tear spinach leaves into bite-size pieces. Crumble bleu cheese over spinach; add onion rings. Toss with desired amount of dressing.

DEFROSTING CHART

1. Remove packaging and place meat in utensil to be used for cooking.

2. Defrost on 30% (medium-low). If using 50% (medium), use less time than below and watch food carefully so parts will not begin to cook.

3. Using small pieces of aluminum foil, shield edges of food if they become warm to the touch and remainder of food is still frozen.

4. After defrosting large or thick foods, allow standing time for center to complete defrosting.

5. Defrost foods completely before cooking.

MEATS	MINUTES PER POUND	SPECIAL INSTRUCTIONS
GROUND MEATS Beef, Pork, Lamb, Bulk Sausage	7-8	After 5 minutes, remove defrosted portion. Repeat every 2 minutes, breaking up remaining chunk.
ROASTS 2″ thick and over	9-11	Turn over and rotate 2-3 times. Shield where necessary. Let stand 15 minutes before cooking.
STEAKS	7-8	Turn over once. Shield. Let stand 10 minutes before cooking.
CHOPS, CUTLETS, MEAT PATTIES, SPARERIBS	6-7	Separate pieces when possible and rearrange.
LIVER	5-7	Remove from carton midway through defrosting. After defrost time, separate and rinse in cold water.
HOT DOGS, SAUSAGE LINKS, LUNCH MEATS	4-5	Make slit in package. Turn over midway through defrosting.
BACON	3-4	Make slit in package. Turn over mid-way through defrosting.
POULTRY		
CHICKEN PIECES	5-7	Separate pieces when possible. Turn over and rearrange. Soak in cool water after defrost time.
WHOLE CHICKEN, CORNISH HENS	6-8	Shield drumsticks and wings. Turn over twice. Remove giblets and neck when possible. Soak in cold water after defrost time.
TURKEY BREAST	7-8	Turn once. Let stand 15 minutes.
WHOLE TURKEY	3-4	See whole chicken above.
SEAFOOD		
FISH FILLETS	8	Flip over midway through. Run under cool water to finish defrosting.
FISH STEAKS	5-6	Turn once. Shield if necessary.
WHOLE FISH	7	Shield tail. Turn twice. Rinse with cool water.
SHRIMPS, SCALLOPS	3-4	Separate pieces after half of defrosting. Run under cool water to finish.
CRAB MEAT	7-8	Defrost in carton. Set carton in cool water to finish defrosting.

Note: To speed up defrosting, microwave on high 1 minute per pound of food. Finish on 30%. Will take less additional time than chart above.

This chart is reprinted from *Microwave Know-How*, a microwave cookbook by CiCi Williamson and Ann Steiner.

"MANAGING" THE KITCHEN

Would you run an office without a telephone or typewriter? Hardly. Can you manage a kitchen without the proper utensils? Some people try, but lacking the required dishes, implements, or measurers definitely contributes to recipe failure.

There are 8 basic utensils that will enable you to microwave almost all the recipes in this book. Most of these utensils can be used in a regular oven as well as in a microwave, and they will still be in use long after the final payment is made on your mortgage! When you consider the cost of groceries today, these utensils are a bargain. For an investment of under $60, you can buy the items listed below. Look in your kitchen. You may have some of them already. If you don't want to buy the ones you lack all at once, purchase one each week until you have them all:

Glass Batter Bowls We use these more frequently than any other utensil, because you can measure ingredients in them, use them as mixing bowls, and then microwave the food in them. If you only want one size, buy the 2-qt. Once you see how handy it is, you'll probably want to add the 1-qt size.

2-Qt Rectangular Glass or Plastic Dish Meat, fish, poultry, lasagne, and cakes (to name a few) can be cooked in this dish.

Bacon or Meat Rack Besides meats, this rack can be used for reheating sandwiches or for cooking several individual items at the same time, such as appetizers.

Casserole Dishes You should have both 1- and 3-qt sizes. The best shape for microwaving is round. These can be either plastic, glass (such as Pyrex), or glass ceramic (such as Corning Ware).

Most of these have lids, but plastic wrap can also be used as a cover. Appetizers, entrees, vegetables, and rice will cook in these.

Dishwasher-Safe Plastic Colander We use this most for cooking ground meats so that the fat can drain as it microwaves. It needs to be labeled "dishwasher safe," because if the plastic can withstand the heat of a dishwasher drying element, it will not melt when meat is cooked in it. The colander is also useful for washing vegetables and draining spaghetti.

4-Qt Plastic Pot You can't make a big batch of spaghetti sauce, chili, stew, or soup without one of these.

Glass Baking Dishes Microwaving pies and cakes in these is only the beginning. They're used for *everything!* A 9-in pie plate, an 8-in square dish, a 9-in round baking dish, and a 9 x 5 x 3-in loaf pan are needed.

Four (6-oz) Glass Custard Cups Poach eggs, cook artichokes, or microwave small amounts of any food in these.

If you are not sure whether a cooking utensil you already have is safe to use in the microwave, put the empty utensil into the oven. Fill a 1-cup glass measure with cool water and place it in the oven so that it is not touching the utensil to be tested. **MW on high** for 1 to 1½ minutes. If the water is warm and the utensil is cool, it is microwave safe. If the utensil feels warm, do not use it for microwave cooking because it has some metallic content.

Other utensils that are nice to have include a 12-in round tray, a microwave food cover for reheating, and a Bundt pan.

Besides utensils to cook in, a well-managed kitchen must have the following food preparation utensils and small implements:

THE FOOD PROCESSOR

"Zip and zap" to make food preparation easier! The food processor and the microwave oven make a dynamic duo to help you get food on the table faster.

People don't realize that most food processor bowls are microwave safe. After you have chopped or processed items, remove the steel blade, cover the bowl with plastic wrap, and microwave the food. This is especially handy if you need to sauté chopped vegetables, such as onion, celery, or green pepper.

If your food processor has a plastic mixing blade, it can be left in the bowl when microwaving. Use this method for softening cream cheese or butter which is to be blended with other ingredients.

If your processor bowl has a metal handle or magnetic parts, do not use it in the microwave oven. Check your owner's manual. Most bowls have a metal spring in the plastic handle, which is part of the safety-locking mechanism.

PRIME MINISTER BRIAN MULRONEY'S VEAL SOUR SOUP

Serves 4 to 8

1 lb veal stew meat, cut into small chunks
8 cups hottest tap water
3 Tbsp instant beef bouillon granules, or 10 beef bouillon cubes
½ tsp coarsely ground black pepper
2 fresh tomatoes, chopped
1 medium potato, peeled and chopped
1 medium onion, sliced
1 rib celery, thinly sliced
3 cauliflower florets, chopped
1 green bell pepper, seeded and chopped
¼ cup corn oil
3 Tbsp all-purpose flour
½ tsp paprika
2 tbsp sour cream
1 Tbsp fresh lemon juice

Canadian Prime Minister Mulroney used a veal knuckle in his conventional recipe. We substituted veal stew meat when we converted his recipe so that it would be faster and easier to make in a microwave.

1 Put veal and 1 cup of water in a 4-qt. casserole. Cover with lid or plastic wrap and **MW on high** for 4 to 5 minutes, stirring midway through cooking. Using a slotted spoon, remove veal.

2 To the same casserole, add 3 cups of water, instant bouillon granules, and pepper. Add tomatoes, potato, onion, celery, and cauliflower. Re-cover and **MW on high** for 20 minutes. Add bell pepper, re-cover, and **MW on high** for 10 minutes.

3 Set a large strainer across a 2-qt. casserole or mixing bowl. Pour soup through strainer. Save cooked vegetables for other uses. Pour strained soup liquid back into 4-qt. casserole. Add reserved veal and remaining 4 cups hot water.

4 Combine oil, flour, and paprika. Using a whisk, stir mixture into soup. Cover and **MW on high** for 10 minutes. Whisk sour cream and lemon juice into soup. Just before serving, reheat soup on 70% (medium-high) or use temperature probe set for 160°F.

Measuring Utensils
Glass measuring cups
Graduated measuring cups
Set of measuring spoons

Small Implements
Bottle opener
Can opener
Carving knife
Chef's knife
Corkscrew
Grater
Ladle
Meat fork
Metal spatula
Pancake turner
Paring knife
Rubber spatulas
Slotted spoon
Tongs
Vegetable peeler
Whisk (stainless steel)
Wooden mallet
Wooden spoons

Food Preparation Utensils
Mixing bowls in various
   sizes
Food scale for weighing
Flour sifter

Electric Appliances
Mixer
Toaster
Either a blender or a
   food processor

MICROWAVING T.V. DINNERS

When people began cooking with microwaves, it was thought that nothing made of metal should be placed in a microwave oven. On January 15, 1985, Underwriters Laboratories (UL), the most respected consumer safety and product testing facility in the world, published test results supporting a different opinion. They tested aluminum T. V. dinner trays and concluded, "No apparent risk exists when packaged frozen food in aluminum containers is heated in microwave ovens."

A sampling of microwave oven manufacturers we contacted showed that microwaving of fro-zen T. V. dinners in their aluminum trays was possible. One recommendation was to remove the aluminum foil cover from the frozen dinner, and place the tray back into its cardboard box for microwaving. Another suggested method was to put waxed paper over the uncovered food and discard the box.

Even though using aluminum frozen food trays will not damage your oven if done so correctly, there are 2 reasons why we don't recommend it. First, since metal reflects microwaves, the waves cannot penetrate the bottom and sides of the tray. The frozen foods will defrost and reheat only from the top and therefore the cooking is uneven.

Second, sitting down at the dinner table to stare into a disposable compartmentalized aluminum tray has neither appetite appeal nor attractiveness. Frozen dinners will look more appealing and cook evenly if microwaved on a dinner plate. You might even be able to fool some people into thinking it was a home-cooked meal!

It is very easy to transfer the frozen food from its foil tray to a plate. Turn the tray upside down and "pop" the food out as if it were ice cubes. Cover the dinner plate with plastic wrap or a microwave food cover. **MW on 70% (medium-high)** until heated through, stirring or rearranging foods midway.

Some foods contained in those commercial packaged T. V. dinners should be avoided or handled separately, however. Remove French fries, cake or muffin batters, and other foods that do not microwave well.

Other frozen dinners are packaged on a microwave-safe plate covered with foil and topped by a plastic lid. To heat in the microwave, remove the foil, replace the plastic lid, and **MW on high** according to package directions. Frozen foods packaged in paperboard trays and dishes are micro-wave safe. Microwave as the package directs.

If you have any entrees packaged in rectangular foil dishes that are deeper than ³/₄ in, remove them from the dish before microwaving. Microwave-safe "frozen-food dishes" are just the right size for heating these entrees.

We like to make our own homemade T. V. dinners. Instead of putting leftovers in the refrigerator to be forgotten and gather mold, we freeze them. Use purchased or saved aluminum trays and frozen entree containers as well as microwave-safe reusable T. V. dinner trays with snap-on lids. You can also freeze foods on your dinner plates, if they are the "freezer-to-table" type.

Group foods together which heat evenly in the same amount of time. Do not freeze a raw entree with other pre-cooked foods. We prefer to freeze entrees which have been cooked, because they are faster and easier to defrost and reheat.

Place your main course in the large compartment of a tray. Add frozen vegetables such as peas, corn, or beans to the small compartments without pre-cooking. Spoon the foods evenly into the sections, and fill no higher than the rim, if using an aluminum tray. Seal the tray with heavy-duty aluminum foil. Crimp the foil tightly over the edges of the tray. For extra protection, place the covered tray in a plastic bag, then label with the date and contents. After all, sometimes frozen foods do not resemble anything recognizable!

KEEP YOUR SPIRITS UP!

To stock a basic bar, you need an assortment of liquor, liqueurs, and wines. Many of these can also be used in making the recipes in this book.

LIQUOR
Bourbon
Brandy

Gin
Rum
Vermouth, dry
Vermouth, sweet
Vodka
Whiskey, blended U.S.
Whiskey, Canadian
Whiskey, Irish
Whiskey, Scotch

LIQUEURS
Coffee, such as Kahlua'
Creme de menthe
Fruit flavor

WINES
2 Champagnes (French)
2 Red (Burgundy or
  Bordeaux)
3 White (Alsatian, Rhine, or
  Moselle)
3 Rosé (French, Italian,
  Portuguese)
1 Sherry
1 Port
1 Madeira

TEMPERATURE PROBE

A temperature probe (or food thermometer) probably came with your microwave oven. Even though you can cook all the recipes in this book without one, probes are useful in various ways.

If you set the temperature at 110°F, the probe can measure the proper heating for baby bottles, water for dissolving yeast, and yogurt making. Temperatures of 150° to 160°F. are best for soups, casseroles, and beverages. See other sections of the book for correct meat and poultry temperatures. Since the maximum temperatures measured by your probe are less than 200°F, it cannot be used in jelly or candy making.

The probe consists of a heat-sensing rod attached to a cord which plugs into the oven cavity. Since the accuracy of the probe depends upon its placement within the food, insert it so that its point is in the center of the food. When programmed, the oven microwaves food until the probe senses that the temperature has been reached. At this point, most ovens automatically shut off. Other ovens will maintain the food at the programmed temperature until manually shut off. Due to the carryover cooking characteristic of microwave cooking, the temperature of foods will rise about 10° to 15°F after microwaving.

MEAT COOKING TIMES CHART

An important principle of microwave cooking is that the more food you put into a microwave oven, the longer it takes to cook. If you weigh food on a kitchen scale, you can determine the microwave time for cooking it perfectly.

If you have not been using a scale, you can only guess at the results. Potatoes, for example, may be super spuds one night and disaster duds another!

Different foods require differing amounts of cooking time and also various power levels. Use the following charts for microwaving meats and vegetables.

MEAT	POWER LEVEL	MINUTES PER POUND
Ground beef, lamb	100%	5 to 6
Ground pork sausage	100%	6 to 7
Tender beef roasts		
Eye of round	50%	8 to 9
Tenderloin	50%	9 to 11
Standing rib	50%	11 to 13
Rolled rib	50%	13 to 15
Sirloin tip	50%	15 to 17
Chuck roast stew meat	30%	20
Pork tenderloin	70%	8 to 10
Pork chops	50%	16 to 18
Ham, precooked	50%	10
Ham, raw	50%	16 to 18
Chicken, turkey	100%	6 to 7
Cornish hens	70%	8 to 9
Fish	100%	3 to 4

This chart is reprinted from *MicroQuick!*, a microwave cookbook by CiCi Williamson and Ann Steiner.

DO YOU MEASURE UP?

It is absolutely essential to the success of a recipe that the correct amount and type of ingredients be used. There is a crucial relationship among the ingredients which provides the intended chemical reaction during cooking. Accurate measuring is especially important in microwave cooking, where the required cooking time is directly proportional to the amounts of ingredients being used.

Is a cup a cup? Some cups are not! There are cups made especially for measuring liquids, and some that are for dry ingredients. A coffee cup is neither of these, and should never be used for measuring.

Every kitchen must have the proper measuring equipment:

- 2 or 3 glass measuring cups (1-, 2-, or 4-cup sizes)
- A set of 4 graduated measuring cups (¼-, ⅓-, ½-, and 1-cup sizes)
- A set of measuring spoons (¼-, ½-, and 1-tsp, and 1 Tbsp)

Measure liquids in glass measuring cups that have a handle and a pouring spout. If you look at the red markings on the side of the 1-cup measure, you will notice that the 8-oz mark (1 cup) is at least ½-in below the top of the cup. This extra space is to prevent the liquid from spilling over the top.

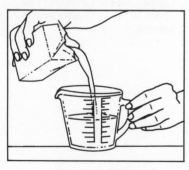

To measure liquid in a glass cup, set it on the counter. Slowly

pour the liquid into the cup until you think it has reached the desired line. Then bend over and look through the side of the cup to see if the liquid is to the correct line. Add more liquid or pour off the excess until it "measures up!"

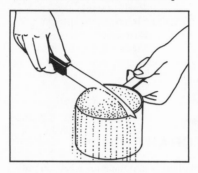

Since the 1-cup mark in a glass measure is below the top, dry ingredients cannot be measured accurately in it. To measure dry ingredients, use the graduated measuring cups. These are designed to be filled to overflowing, and then leveled across the top with the straight edge of a spatula or knife. Do not measure liquids in these cups because liquids cannot be leveled with a knife. The cup would either overflow, or contain less than the amount needed.

When measuring flour, do not scoop the cup into the container of flour because it will pack more into the cup than is needed. The correct way to measure flour is to spoon it lightly into the cup until it overflows, and then level it off.

It is correct to scoop the cup into the container of granulated sugar, however, because it doesn't pack the way flour does. Fill it to overflowing and level. Brown sugar and shortening are measured in a different way. Pack them into the cup before leveling. If packed correctly, brown sugar will hold its shape when the cup is emptied (see page 119).

Another way to measure shortening is by the water-displacement method. If a recipe requires ⅔ cup of shortening, place ⅓ cup cold water in a glass measuring

cup. Add shortening until the water level reaches the 1-cup line. Pour off water and add the shortening to the recipe.

Margarine or butter can also be measured by the markings on the sticks. One stick equals 8 Tbsp, or ½ cup. For ⅓ cup, use 5⅓ Tbsp. If your package does not have these markings on each stick, measure as for shortening.

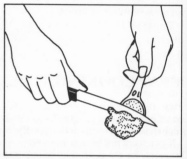

Measuring spoons are used for either liquid or dry ingredients. Fill and level dry ingredients as you would if using the graduated cups. If measuring liquids, pour just to the top of the spoon without letting it overflow.

MICROWAVE OVEN CLEANING

When is the last time you cleaned your microwave oven? Because spatters do not burn in microwave ovens the way they do in conventional gas or electric ovens, many people overlook them. However, each time you microwave something, check for spills or spatters, and clean them up immediately. This eliminates a more difficult cleaning task later.

When food particles are allowed to remain or accumulate in your oven, they can become spoiled and rancid, causing unpleasant odors. The accumulation of food soil around the frame or on the door can interfere with the safety seal on the door. Microwaves are attracted to food and can't distinguish between stale and fresh food. Therefore, cooking can be slowed considerably when the stale food robs some of the microwave energy from the food to be cooked.

When cleaning the control panel, it's especially important not to use excess water, which can drip behind knobs and moldings into the motor housing. Don't allow grease to build up on the touch panels because this makes them difficult to program. To clean control panels, wipe with a cloth dampened with water or mild detergent.

The door and interior of an oven should also be cleaned with a mild detergent or a solution of 4 Tbsp baking soda dissolved in 1 qt of warm water. After washing, rinse and wipe dry. On stainless-steel interiors, we prefer an ammonia-based glass cleaner (such as Windex) to remove the noticeable streakiness left from the soap residue. Clean the inside of the oven frequently using a mild detergent and wipe with paper towels or a damp cloth. No harsh detergents, abrasives, or scouring pads should be used.

To loosen soil and make interiors easier to clean, boil a cup of water in a bowl or 2-cup liquid measure for 3 to 4 minutes. Leave the door closed. Steam will condense on the oven interior and make the food soil much easier to remove. Wipe out with a paper towel, soft cloth, or sponge.

Foods such as tomato paste or berry juice can leave stains, especially on interiors with painted acrylic surfaces. Dampen a dishcloth with bleach and water, and place it on the stain. Microwave the dishcloth on high until warm, not hot. Wipe oven cavity with cloth. You can also rub the stain with Bon Ami cleanser or a paste of baking soda and water. If this doesn't work, make a paste of Soft Scrub or Comet and water. Rinse and dry.

If the interior painted surfaces have become chipped or burned, several microwave manufacturers have acrylic touch-up paint kits available from their "parts departments." You can also have the paint retouched by an authorized repair service person.

What do you do if your oven is emitting unpleasant food odors? One way to eradicate them is to combine the juice and peel of a lemon with 1 cup of water. Boil on high for 5 minutes, then dampen a cloth with the lemon water and wipe the oven. One manufacturer suggests washing the walls with water and baking soda. Another idea is to place an opened box of baking soda in the microwave oven for 24 hours.

Many microwave ovens now have removeable glass trays as their cooking surfaces. It is very easy to remove these and wash them in the sink. Just be careful not to break one, because they are expensive to replace! Food residue or stains on a ceramic floor can be removed with a paste of baking soda or a special ceramic glass cleaner such as Corning Ceramic Conditioner or Barkeeper's Friend.

Microwave-convection ovens can be cleaned by the same methods given earlier. Soft Scrub or Bon Ami can be used on stainless-steel areas, and plastic or nylon scouring sponges, or pads made for use on Teflon or Silverstone-treated cookware, can also be used.

Under no circumstances should you remove to clean the antenna cover from the ceiling of the microwave oven. If there are metal shelves in the oven, they can be removed and put into the dishwasher. They can also be cleaned inside the oven with mild soap and water. Do not clean them in a self-cleaning conventional oven.

Remember, a clean microwave oven will cook more efficiently. You'll keep it sparkling if you clean as you cook.

HOW BARE IS YOUR CUPBOARD?

Besides having the right utensils and measurers, another way to ensure that the recipes you cook will be a success is to use the correct ingredients. Foods that do not have to be refrigerated or frozen and that keep indefinitely are known as "staples." Inventory your pantry periodically to be sure you always have them. If you notice a particular "staple" running low, write it on your grocery list to buy before you run out. The following staples are those used to make the recipes in this book. Herbs and spices are not included in this list because they are next.

Almonds
Artichoke hearts
Baking powder and baking
    soda
Bamboo shoots
Bouillon, instant beef and
    chicken
Bread crumbs, dry
Broth, canned beef and
    chicken
Brown sugar
Chiles (chopped and
    whole, canned)
Chili sauce
Chocolate, unsweetened &
    semi-sweet
Cocoa
Corn or tortilla chips
Corn syrup, light and dark
Cornstarch
Evaporated milk
Extracts, vanilla and lemon
Flour
French-fried onions
Gelatin, unflavored
Grits
Honey
Ketchup
Kitchen Bouquet
Lasagne noodles
Lemon juice
Liquid Smoke
Mayonnaise
Mushrooms, canned
Mustard, Dijon and regular
Oatmeal
Oil (vegetable cooking oil)
Olive oil
Olives
Pam (non-stick cooking
    spray)
Pasta (dry spaghetti, noodles)

Peanuts
Peppers, canned jalapeños
Pimientos
Raisins
Refried beans
Rice
Shortening, solid (Crisco)
Soup mix, dehydrated
Soy sauce
Stuffing mix, dry
Sugar
Tabasco sauce
Taco sauce
Tomato sauce and paste
Tomatoes, canned
Water chestnuts
Vinegar, cider and white
Wine vinegar (red)
Worcestershire sauce

SPICES ARE THE VARIETY OF LIFE!

Spice up your microwave cooking! Herbs and spices add flavor, color, and appetite appeal to microwaved foods. The only rule is to suit your taste!

According to Tom Burns, executive vice-president of the American Spice Trade Association, the seasonings most purchased by consumers in the United States are black pepper, dehydrated garlic products, and paprika. Our use of herbs has increased dramatically over the past 20 years. For example, in 1964, 42,000 pounds of basil were imported; by 1984, this figure had jumped to more than 3 million pounds.

The following list of spices and herbs includes all those needed to make every recipe in this book. If you are stocking a kitchen for the first time, don't buy all of them at once, because it would be quite an investment. Those most frequently used are designated by an asterisk, and you should buy those first. As you do more cooking, purchase the ones required in new recipes you want to try. Pretty soon, you'll have quite a variety.

If you have never bought herbs and spices, the prices may seem expensive. But consider this: ¹/₂ oz of dried basil can flavor 128 servings of Italian meat sauce; about 1 oz of cinnamon can season 456 slices of apple pie; and 1 oz of ground black pepper can spice 1,440 fried eggs! Dried herbs and spices of highest quality are packed in glass jars, while a less expensive grade is put into cans.

Spices and herbs are on the semi-perishable list. According to McCormick & Co., the largest spice company in the world, if properly stored and used, whole spices will be good 2 to 5 years or longer. Ground spices and leafy herbs will retain their flavoring up to 2 years. When you buy a new seasoning, write the date on the container with a laundry marker. Replace that herb or spice when it reaches its shelf life.

Members of the red pepper family (red pepper, cayenne, chili powder, and paprika) will last 1 year, perhaps 2 if stored in the refrigerator. Dehydrated vegetables will stay fresh for 6 months.

To retain flavor of dried herbs and spices at home, store them in a cool, dark place as far away from heat and moisture as possible. Avoid hanging your spice rack over the range or near a window. Keep spices tightly covered when not in use to hold in freshness. Measuring spoons that dip into the spice or herb jar should be dry and free of any other seasoning or ingredient.

If you want to substitute fresh herbs, use 3 times the amount of dried herbs called for in a recipe.

Allspice
Basil*
Bay leaves*
Caraway seeds
Cayenne pepper*
Celery salt
Chili powder*
Chives, dried
Cinnamon, ground*
Cloves, ground and whole
Coriander, ground

Cumin, ground* and seeds
Dill weed and seeds
Fennel seeds
Garlic, instant minced
Garlic powder*
Ginger, ground*
Italian seasoning
Mustard, dry
Mint
Nutmeg, ground
Onion, instant minced
Onion powder
Oregano*
Paprika*
Parsley flakes
Pepper, black*
Pepper, white*
Poppy seeds
Poultry seasoning
Rosemary
Saffron
Sage
Salt*
Sesame seeds
Thyme
Turmeric

SUBSTITUTION CHART

There's nothing more aggravating than finding that you're out of an ingredient you need to prepare a recipe. If you make a special trip to the supermarket, you'll probably waste the better part of an hour standing in the Express Lane behind a harried lady with 25 items, who is writing a check while above her, the sign clearly reads, "Limit 8 items. Cash only. No checks."

If you're in luck, you may find a substitute on this list for the ingredient you need. If you don't find it on the list, either try a different recipe or get out your car keys!

- **Allspice** 1 tsp equals ¹/₂ tsp ground cinnamon plus ¹/₈ tsp ground cloves.
- **Baking Powder** 1 tsp equals ¹/₃ tsp baking soda plus ¹/₂ tsp cream of tartar (a dry powder on the spice shelf).
- **Bread Crumbs** ¹/₄ cup dry bread crumbs equals ¹/₂ cup soft bread crumbs or 1 slice

bread made into crumbs in a blender or food processor.

- **Broth or Stock** For 1 cup of beef broth, substitute 1 cup hot water plus 2 beef bouillon cubes or 2 tsp instant beef bouillon granules. For chicken broth, substitute 1 cup hot water plus 2 chicken bouillon cubes or 2 tsp instant chicken bouillon granules.

- **Brown Sugar** 1 cup firmly packed equals 1 cup granulated sugar or 1³/₄ cups confectioners sugar. A 1-lb box of brown sugar equals 2¹/₄ firmly packed cups.

- **Butter** equals margarine. 1 cup equals ⁷/₈ cup oil or 14 Tbsp solid shortening (such as Crisco).

- **Buttermilk** 1 cup equals 1 cup plain yogurt. Or place 1 Tbsp white vinegar in a measuring cup and fill with milk to the 1-cup mark; let stand 5 minutes.

- **Cheese** 4 oz equal 1 cup of shredded. Type substitutions:

Cheddar. Colby, Cheshire, Coon, Gloucester, Longhorn, Processed American, Rat Cheese.

Bleu. Gorgonzola, Roquefort, Stilton.

Brie. Bel Paese, Camembert, Corolle, Limberger, Port-Salut.

Cottage. Farmer, Pot, Ricotta.

Cream. Neufchatel, Petit Suisse, Gervais.

Monterey Jack. Mozzarella, Brick, Domestic Swiss, Edam, Gouda, Havarti, Muenster, Provolone.

Parmesan. Romano, Sapsago, aged Asiago.

Swiss. Alpsberg, Appenzeller, Emmentaler, Fontina, Gruyère, Jarlsberg, Switzerland.

- **Chicken** 2 cups cooked chopped chicken or turkey meat equal the amount from a cooked and deboned 3-lb chicken. All types of bone-in raw chicken parts weighing the same are interchangeable. All types of boneless raw poultry weighing the same are interchangeable.

- **Chocolate** 1 oz unsweetened (1 square) equals 3 Tbsp cocoa plus 1 Tbsp butter or margarine; equals 3 Tbsp carob powder plus 2 Tbsp water. Also, 1 oz unsweetened plus 4 tsp sugar equal 1²/₃ oz semi-sweet chocolate.

- **Cracker Crumbs** ³/₄ cup equals 1 cup dry bread crumbs.

- **Cream** (Heavy or Whipping) 1 cup equals ³/₄ cup milk plus ¹/₃ cup butter. (This cannot be whipped.)

- **Cream** (Light or Half & Half) 1 cup equals ⁷/₈ cup milk plus 3 Tbsp butter; or ¹/₂ cup milk plus ¹/₂ cup heavy cream.

- **Cream, Sour** 1 cup equals 1 cup plain yogurt; or 1 cup pureed cottage cheese; or 6 oz cream cheese plus 4 Tbsp milk.

- **Eggs** 2 large eggs equal 3 small eggs; 2 egg yolks equal 1 whole egg.

- **Garlic** 1 fresh medium clove equals ¹/₂ tsp fresh minced or prepared chopped garlic in a jar; or ¹/₈ tsp garlic powder; or ¹/₂ tsp instant minced garlic. Garlic salt is half salt and half garlic powder.

- **Herbs** 1 tsp dried equals 3 tsp fresh.

- **Lemon Juice** 1 fresh lemon yields 2 to 3 Tbsp juice; defrosted frozen lemon juice equals fresh lemon juice; 1 tsp lemon juice equals ¹/₂ tsp vinegar.

- **Milk** 1 cup whole milk equals ¹/₂ cup canned evaporated milk plus ¹/₂ cup water; equals ¹/₃ cup instant nonfat dry milk plus ³/₄ cup water and 2 tsp butter.

- **Mushrooms** 8 oz cooked fresh mushrooms equal 1 can (4-oz) of mushrooms, drained; 8 oz raw fresh mushrooms equal 2¹/₂ cups.

- **Noodles** Cooked noodles can be substituted for the same amount of any other cooked spaghetti or pasta; 4 cups uncooked noodles equal 5 oz. Noodles double in volume when cooked.

- **Oil** (Vegetable Cooking Oil, such as Mazola or Wesson) ¹/₂ cup equals 1 stick margarine.

- **Onion** ¹/₄ cup chopped fresh onion equals 1 Tbsp instant minced onion or ¹/₄ cup frozen chopped onion; 1 medium onion chopped equals about 1 cup.

- **Parsley** 1 tsp dried parsley equals 1 Tbsp chopped fresh parsley.

- **Peppers, Bell** Green bell peppers equal red bell peppers. These are not the same as green chiles, which are hot.

- **Pepper, Cayenne** A pinch of ground red pepper or cayenne equals 2 dashes of Tabasco sauce.

- **Sour Cream** (See Cream, Sour)

- **Sugar** 1 cup granulated equals 1 cup brown sugar or 1³/₄ cups confectioners (powdered) sugar.

- **Tomatoes** 1 can (16 oz), drained, equals 2 cups chopped fresh tomatoes.

- **Tomato Paste** 1 Tbsp equals 1 Tbsp ketchup.

- **Tomato Puree** 1 cup equals ¹/₂ cup tomato paste plus ¹/₂ cup water.

- **Tomato Sauce** 1 cup equals ¹/₂ cup tomato paste plus ¹/₂ cup water.

- **Worcestershire Sauce** 1 tsp equals 1 Tbsp soy sauce plus a dash of hot pepper sauce.

- **Yogurt** 1 cup equals 1 cup buttermilk.

Meals in Micro Time

Most of these recipes can be prepared in about 20 minutes or less. To complete the meal, they need only a salad, bread, or vegetable accompaniment. Included here are traditional American favorites as well as recipes inspired by the authors' international travels. All the ingredients should be available at any large supermarket.

SUNRISE SPECIALS

Don't skip breakfast. Even on hectic mornings, there are a variety of hot, nutritious foods that can be ready in a minute or two with a microwave oven. On leisurely days, you can microwave something more elaborate.

QUICK GRITS

Serves 1

3/4 cup hottest tap water

1/8 tsp salt

3 Tbsp quick grits

1 Tbsp butter or margarine

1 Put water and salt in a microwave-safe bowl. **MW on high** for 1½ to 2 minutes, or until water boils.

2 Stir grits into water gradually. **MW on high** for 1 minute. Stir, then **MW on 50% (medium)** for 1 minute. Stir butter into grits, and let stand 1 minute.

QUICK OATMEAL

Serves 1

2/3 cup hottest tap water

1/8 tsp salt

1/3 cup quick oats

1 Combine water, salt, and oats in a microwave-safe bowl; stir well. **MW on high** for 1 minute.

2 Stir, then **MW on high** for 1 to 2 minutes. Stir and let stand 1 minute.

INSTANT CREAM OF WHEAT

Serves 1

3/4 cup hottest tap water

2½ Tbsp instant cream of wheat

1 Combine water and cream of wheat in a microwave-safe bowl; stir well. **MW on high** for 1 minute.

2 Stir, then **MW on high** for 1 to 2 minutes. Stir and let stand 1 minute.

NOTE
To make 2 or more servings, do not use individual bowls. Put ingredients into a 1 or 2-qt glass batter bowl, depending on desired number of servings. Increase cooking times by three-fourths for each additional serving.

SCRAMBLED EGGS

1 Use 1 Tbsp of milk for each egg, and beat with the desired amount of salt and pepper in a glass measuring cup.

2 Cover with plastic wrap and **MW on high** for 30 to 45 seconds per egg, or to desired doneness. Stir at least once or twice during cooking.

POACHED EGGS

1 For each egg that you want to microwave, put ¼ cup water and ¼ tsp white vinegar into the same number of 6-oz custard cups. Arrange custard cups containing water mixture in a circle on a microwave-safe plate, tray, or rotating turntable. Cover all with 1 piece of plastic wrap. **MW on high** for 1 to 2 minutes, or until water boils.

2 Remove plastic wrap and crack one egg into each cup of water. Puncture each yolk with a fork; replace plastic wrap. Turning tray halfway around midway through cooking, **MW on 50% (medium)** for 45 to 60 seconds per egg. Let stand to desired doneness. Remove from water using a slotted spoon.

SHIRRED (BAKED) OR HARD-COOKED EGGS

1 Break each egg you want to bake or hard cook into a 6-oz custard cup. Pierce each yolk 2 times with a fork.

2 Arrange custard cups as in Poached Eggs, above. Cover all with 1 piece of plastic wrap. Turn tray halfway around midway through cooking. For baked eggs, **MW on 50% (medium)** for 45 to 60 seconds per egg. For hard-cooked eggs, **MW on 50%** for 1½ to 2 minutes per egg.

MAJOR KELLY'S MAYDAY

Serves 4

1 lb ground beef
¼ cup chopped onion
7 Tbsp all-purpose flour
2 tsp dry brown gravy mix (part of a ¾-oz envelope)
1 tsp salt
¼ tsp black pepper
1 Tbsp tomato paste
2¼ cups milk
1 tsp Worcestershire sauce
8 slices toast
parsley flakes

"MAYDAY" is the modern radio version of the telegraph signal "S.O.S.," which is the military nickname for this recipe!

1 Place a dishwasher-safe plastic colander into a 2-qt casserole dish. Crumble ground beef into colander and sprinkle onion on top of beef. **MW on high** for 3 minutes.

2 Use a wooden spoon to stir meat and break up chunks. **MW on high** for 3 minutes, or until meat is no longer pink.

3 Remove colander of meat and set aside. Pour grease

from casserole into a can, and later when it has solidified, throw it away. Transfer meat and onion from colander into same casserole. Into the meat, stir flour, gravy mix, salt, and pepper until well blended. Stir in tomato paste.

4 Pour milk and Worcestershire sauce into meat mixture. Stir well. Cover casserole with glass lid or plastic wrap. **MW on high** for 5 minutes. Stir well. Replace cover and **MW on high** for 3 minutes, or until mixture thickens. Spoon over toast and sprinkle with parsley flakes to add color.

NOTE

Refrigerate any leftover sauce. Do not freeze because milk in sauce will curdle. You'll also have leftover tomato paste. After removing 1 Tbsp of tomato paste for the recipe, scrape remaining tomato paste from can into a plastic sandwich bag. Close bag with a twist tie, and freeze to use in other recipes.

SNACKS

Move beyond cold sandwiches to these hot snacks, fixed in a flash.

HAMBURGERS

When buying beef to make hamburgers, regular ground beef is the best bargain. According to Dr. Russell Cross of the United States Department of Agriculture, "There is practically no difference in cooked hamburgers, whether made from extra-lean or regular ground beef, except that hamburgers made from regular beef are juicier and a bit tastier." They contain almost identical amounts of protein. As hamburgers are grilled or microwaved, regular ground beef will lose fat while extra-lean ground beef will lose water.

If you are going to freeze ground beef to make hamburgers later, shape the meat into patties on squares of waxed paper. Meat patties will defrost much faster than a block of ground beef. Stack the patties according to the number you need for a meal, and wrap for the freezer.

HOW TO DEFROST HAMBURGERS

Remove freezer wrapping and separate the patties by wedging a dinner knife between the layers of waxed paper. Place patties on a microwave meat or bacon rack. If you will be cooking the hamburgers immediately, you can defrost the patties on high power, allowing 45 to 60 seconds per patty. Rotate rack midway through defrosting; let stand to complete defrosting.

An easier way to defrost hamburger patties is to transfer them from the freezer to the refrigerator the evening before, or early in the morning. By the following dinnertime, they will defrost themselves.

INDOOR HAMBURGERS

It's impossible to beat hamburgers cooked outdoors on the grill. But what do you do if it rains, the fire won't start, or the gas grill is out of commission? Microwave ovens to the rescue! Four hamburgers can be done in 6 to 7 minutes, and they'll taste good, too.

MICROWAVING ON A RACK

Hamburgers can be microwaved on a microwave meat or bacon rack. If using this method, apply "cosmetics" so that the patties will have an appealing color. Brush the raw patties with Kitchen Bouquet or microwave browning sauce, or moisten and sprinkle them with Micro Shake.

Place patties on a meat rack and cover loosely with waxed paper. We like to microwave hamburger patties on 70% power to minimize shrinkage. For 1 lb (4 patties), **MW on 70% (medium-high)** for 5 to 6 minutes, turning each patty halfway around after 3 minutes. Let stand 2 minutes before serving.

MICROWAVING IN A BROWNING DISH

A browning dish is a Corning Ware utensil with a special metal oxide painted on the bottom. Preheat the empty browning dish in the microwave oven according to manufacturer's instructions for the size you own. Using a pancake turner, press the raw patties onto the preheated browning dish to sear and brown. For 1 lb (4 patties) **MW on high** for 1½ minutes. Turn patties over and **MW on high** for 1½ to 2½ minutes, or until almost done. Let stand 2 minutes.

HAMBURGER HEROS

Serves 2

¾ lb ground beef

2 tsp Worcestershire sauce

salt and pepper

Kitchen Bouquet or Micro Shake

⅓ cup tomato sauce

¼ cup chili sauce

½ tsp wine vinegar

¼ tsp Liquid Smoke

½ tsp dried oregano

¼ tsp chili powder

2 hero sandwich buns

2 thin slices red onion, in rings

¼ cup grated Cheddar cheese

1 Mix ground beef, 1 tsp Worcestershire sauce, salt, and pepper. Divide mixture in half and pat each into a rectangular meat patty to fit a hero sandwich bun. To give patties an attractive brown appearance, sprinkle with Micro Shake or color with Kitchen Bouquet.

2 Place patties on a microwave meat rack. **MW on high** for 5 to 6 minutes, or until meat is desired doneness. Let stand.

3 In a 1-cup glass measure, combine tomato sauce, chili sauce, remaining tsp Worcestershire sauce, vinegar, Liquid Smoke, oregano, and chili powder. Cover with plastic wrap and **MW on high** for 1 to 2 minutes, or until hot.

4 To assemble heros, place cooked meat patties on buns, spoon sauce over meat, and top with onion rings and cheese. **MW on high** until cheese melts.

REHEATING HAMBURGERS

Another use for your microwave oven is reheating cooked hamburgers. We do not recommend reheating an assembled hamburger because the meat juices will make the bun soggy, but you can reheat the patty and bun separately. To reheat 4 hamburger buns without meat, wrap in paper towels and place on a rack. **MW on high** for 25 to 30 seconds. To reheat patties, put them on a plate and **MW on 70% (medium-high)** for 30 seconds per patty.

If you can grill hamburgers outdoors, undercook an extra batch and freeze the individual patties between squares of waxed paper. When you need a meal in a hurry, separate the number of cooked patties you need, and **MW on 70%** until defrosted and heated thoroughly. They will taste as charcoaled as the day you grilled them!

HOT DOGS IN BUNS

Tough, chewy buns and lukewarm hot dogs. Does this sound like what has emerged from your microwave oven? Some people think it is possible

to heat a hot dog in a bun and have them both come out right. We don't.

It takes longer to heat meat than it does bread, so we recommend microwaving the meat first, and then heating it briefly in its bun.

1 Before microwaving any hot dog or fully cooked sausage, pierce it several times with a fork so that steam can vent. **MW on high** for 30 to 40 seconds.

2 Place hot dog in bun. (Do not spread with mustard, ketchup, or other condiments, because they will make the bun soggy.) Wrap hot dog and bun in a paper towel or napkin. **MW on high** for 15 to 20 seconds.

3 Add favorite condiments to heated hot dog in bun, and serve. If you like chili on your hot dog, microwave the chili in a small dish before spooning it on heated hot dog. Add shredded cheese and chopped onion, if desired.

DEFROSTING HOT DOG OR HAMBURGER BUNS

1 Remove the metal twist-tie from the plastic bag and slip a paper towel between the buns and the plastic bag, both top and bottom. This absorbs the melting ice crystals and prevents the buns from becoming soggy.

2 Place bag on a microwave rack. For a package of 8 hamburger buns, **MW on 30% (medium-low)** for 2½ to 3 minutes. Rotate package top to bottom midway through defrosting. Redistribute each layer of 4 buns so that the least defrosted areas are moved to the outside.

3 Separate buns and let stand to finish defrosting. If you microwave bread products too long, they will be tough and chewy.

PIZZA ROLLS

Serves 3

1 can (8-oz) tomato sauce

1 tsp Italian seasoning

¼ tsp dried basil

⅛ tsp garlic powder

3 French-style rolls (3-oz), split in half lengthwise

2 oz thinly sliced pepperoni

1½ cups shredded Mozzarella cheese

1 Combine tomato sauce, Italian seasoning, basil, and garlic powder in a 1-cup glass measure. **MW on high** for 1½ minutes, or until heated through.

2 Spread sauce on cut-side of each roll. Distribute pepperoni slices over top of sauce. Sprinkle ¼ cup of cheese on top of each pizza roll. Place 3 rolls on a paper-lined microwave roasting or bacon rack. **MW on high** for 1½ to 2 minutes, rotating rack midway through heating. Repeat with remaining 3 rolls.

NOTE
Assembled but unheated rolls may be wrapped individually in plastic wrap and frozen. Unwrap the frozen roll and place on a paper towel-lined microwave roasting or bacon rack. For each roll, **MW on high** for 1 minute, or until heated through, rotating rack midway through heating.

MICROWAVING PIZZA

Conventionally, pizza is baked in a very hot oven. The heat makes a crisp crust, and the only way to obtain a crisp crust in the microwave oven is to use a browning dish or tray, or a special pizza crisper made for the microwave oven. These browners have a metallic oxide paint on the bottom that attracts the microwave energy when preheated without any food on them. The surface of the browner gets extremely hot, and when food is placed on it and microwaved, the bottom of the food browns and becomes crisp.

Unless you plan to prepare a lot of pizza in your microwave oven, we wouldn't advise purchasing an expensive utensil for this purpose. An alternative is to buy frozen pizza that comes in a package labelled "crisp crust." There are others made especially for microwave reheating.

If you plan to make your own homemade pizza crust, use the microwave oven to speed the rising of the yeast dough. Remember, however, that microwaved raw pizza dough will not become crisp and brown. We don't recommend baking the raw pizza dough in a microwave oven.

Leftover pieces of pizza can be quickly reheated in the microwave oven. Space individual slices about 1 in apart on a paper-towel-lined microwave bacon rack. **MW on high** approximately 45 to 60 seconds per slice, depending upon size. Let stand briefly, then serve.

ITALIAN HOAGIES

Serves 4

4 submarine sandwich buns or hard onion buns, cut in half

8 slices salami, cut in half

4 slices Provolone cheese, cut in half

8 green bell pepper rings

Thousand Island salad dressing

1 Split buns and arrange salami and cheese to fit on bottom halves of buns. Top with bell pepper. Place bottom buns on a paper towel on a microwave meat or bacon rack. **MW on high** until cheese melts.

2 Drizzle salad dressing on top bun and place over bottoms of buns. **MW on high** for 30 to 40 seconds.

PHILLY STEAK SANDWICHES

Serves 2

1 medium onion, thinly sliced

1 Tbsp bacon drippings (optional)

4 frozen thin beef sandwich steaks, about 2 oz each

2 submarine sandwich buns, split

bottled steak sauce

1 Place onion in a 1-qt round casserole. Add bacon drippings, if desired. Cover with plastic wrap and **MW on high** for 3½ to 4 minutes, or until onion is desired softness. Remove onion from casserole.

2 While still frozen, use a large knife to cut each steak into 4 crosswise strips. Arrange frozen strips overlapping in a wreath configuration in same casserole. Re-cover and **MW on high** for 4 to 5 minutes, stirring and rearranging strips midway through cooking.

3 Divide cooked steak between the 2 buns and drizzle with steak sauce. Arrange onion over steak. Spread top bun with more steak sauce and place on top of steak and onion. Set sandwiches on a paper towel on a microwave meat or bacon rack. **MW on high** for 30 to 40 seconds, or until heated through.

QUESADILLA

Serves 1

2 corn tortillas

¼ cup shredded Longhorn or Monterey Jack cheese

1 Tbsp mild taco sauce

1 tsp chopped green chile

vegetable oil

1 Place 1 tortilla on plate. Sprinkle with cheese and dot with taco sauce and chile. Place another tortilla on top.

2 Oil top tortilla lightly. Cover with a "micro-cover" or another plate. **MW on high** for 1 minute, or until cheese is melted.

3 Cut into 4 wedges for serving.

NOTE
A "micro-cover" is a plastic reheating dome which is turned upside down over the food on a plate. The edge of the bowl sits on the rim of the plate so that it doesn't touch the food.

EASY ENCHILADAS

Serves 6

1 lb ground beef

1 cup chopped onion

1 Tbsp chili powder

1 tsp ground cumin

1 can (8-oz) tomato sauce

¼ cup water

12 corn tortillas

2 Tbsp oil

2 cups shredded Cheddar cheese, about 8 oz

1 can (10-oz) enchilada sauce

1 Place a dishwasher-safe plastic colander into a 2-qt casserole. Crumble ground beef into colander and sprinkle ½ cup onion on top. **MW on high** for 3 minutes.

2 Use a wooden spoon to stir meat and break up chunks. **MW on high** for 3 minutes, or until meat is no longer pink. Pour grease from casserole into a can to discard later. Transfer meat into same casserole.

3 Stir chili powder and cumin into meat. Add ½ can of tomato sauce and ¼ cup water to meat. **MW on high** for 3 to 4 minutes.

4 Put a damp paper towel on a plate large enough to hold tortillas. Working with 6 tortillas at a time, rub 1 side of each with ½ tsp of oil and stack (like pancakes) on damp paper towel. Fold corners of towel over stack. Put an equal size plate upside down over the tortillas. **MW on high** for 1½ minutes.

5 Set aside 1 cup of cheese to top the enchiladas. To assemble, spoon ¼ cup of meat mixture down center of each heated tortilla and sprinkle with cheese. Roll up and place seam-side down in a 2-qt rectangular dish. Repeat heating and assembling remaining tortillas.

6 Mix remaining tomato sauce with enchilada sauce and pour evenly over top of enchiladas. Sprinkle with reserved cheese and remaining ½ cup chopped onion. Cover with plastic wrap. **MW on high** for 10 to 12 minutes, or until heated through.

CHARLEY IN BLANKETS

Serves 3

1 package (10-oz) frozen chopped broccoli

1 can (10¾-oz) condensed cream of mushroom soup

1 cup milk

1 can (6½-oz) tuna, drained

1 cup shredded Cheddar cheese

1 can (2.8-oz) French-fried onions

6 small flour tortillas

1 Place package of frozen broccoli on a paper towel on floor of microwave oven. **MW on high** for 5 to 6 minutes. Drain water from box and place broccoli in a small bowl.

2 In a 4-cup glass measure, mix soup and milk. Pour ¾ cup of soup mixture into bowl with broccoli. Set remaining soup aside. Add tuna, ½ cup cheese, and ½ can of onions to broccoli; mix.

3 Divide broccoli mixture evenly onto the tortillas. Roll up each tortilla and place seam side down in a 2-qt rectangular dish. Pour remaining soup over tortillas. Sprinkle with remaining cheese and onions. Do not cover. **MW on high** for 10 minutes, rotating dish after 5 minutes of cooking.

EASY MEALS

SALMON AND RICE MULLIGAN

Serves 4

2 Tbsp butter or margarine

2 Tbsp all-purpose flour

1½ cups milk

1 tsp salt

¼ tsp black pepper

⅛ tsp cayenne pepper

1 cup shredded sharp Cheddar cheese

2½ cups cooked rice

1 can (15½-oz) salmon, drained

paprika

1 Place butter in a 4-cup glass measure. **MW on high** for 30 seconds, or until melted. Using a wire whisk, stir in flour. Gradually whisk in milk, salt, pepper, and cayenne pepper. Stirring with whisk every 2 minutes, **MW on high** for 5 to 6 minutes, or until mixture thickens. Stir in cheese until it melts.

2 Spread half of rice in the bottom of a 2-qt round casserole. Remove skin and bones from salmon. Flake half of salmon onto rice. Pour half of cheese sauce mixture over salmon. Repeat layers of remaining rice, salmon, and cheese sauce. Sprinkle with paprika. **MW on high** for 6 minutes, or until casserole is hot throughout.

AL WAXMAN'S ORANGE GINGER CHICKEN

Serves 4

¹/₃ cup orange juice

1 tsp cornstarch

1 Tbsp corn oil

1 Tbsp soy sauce

1 Tbsp honey

¹/₂ tsp minced fresh ginger

1 tsp chopped fresh cilantro (Chinese parsley)

1 lb boneless chicken breasts

1 orange

¹/₄ cup roasted cashews

3 cups cooked rice

Al Waxman is a popular Canadian actor. Here's his favorite way to use his microwave oven.

1 In a 2-qt rectangular glass dish, combine orange juice and cornstarch. Add oil, soy sauce, honey, and ginger. **MW on high** for 30 to 45 seconds; stir well. Add cilantro.

2 Cut chicken into thin strips about 2 by ¹/₄ inch. (This is easy to do if chicken is partially frozen.) Stir chicken into sauce mixture. Cover with heavy plastic wrap. **MW on high** 4 to 6 minutes, stirring after each 2 minutes.

3 Grate zest from orange rind; set aside. Peel and seed orange; separate into segments.

Cut each segment in half. Add them to the chicken; re-cover. **MW on high** for 1 to 2 minutes or until heated.

4 Just before serving, sprinkle cashews and orange zest on top of chicken. Serve over rice.

FRANK AUGUSTYN'S SPEEDY STEAK KABOBS

Serves 2 to 3

¹/₄ cup corn oil

2 Tbsp wine vinegar

2 Tbsp soy sauce

1 clove garlic, cut in slivers

2 tsp chopped fresh parsley

¹/₄ teaspoon dried marjoram

1 lb boneless sirloin steak, cut in 1-in cubes

¹/₂ green bell pepper, cut into 8 chunks

cherry tomatoes

fresh mushrooms, cleaned

canned pineapple chunks, drained

1 jar (6-oz) marinated artichoke hearts, drained

Frank Augustyn is principal dancer with the National Ballet of Canada. He has given us one of his choice microwave recipes.

1 In a bowl large enough to hold the meat, combine oil, vinegar, soy sauce, garlic, parsley, and marjoram. Add steak cubes and marinate for 30 to 60 minutes.

2 Thread steak onto 4 to 6 bamboo 8-in skewers, alternating with the assorted vegetables. Arrange kabobs in a 2-qt rectangular dish. Spoon a little of the marinade over the kabobs. Cover with waxed paper.

3 **MW on high** for 3 minutes. Exchange position of skewers near the outside of the dish with those in the center.

Re-cover and **MW on high** for 2 to 3 minutes or until desired doneness.

NOTE

If you do not have marjoram, substitute half the amount each of dried mint and oregano. Raw bell peppers will still be quite crisp after microwaving with other food on skewers. If you do not like crisp pepper, put the chunks in a 2-cup glass measure, cover with plastic wrap, and **MW on high** for 1 to 2 minutes before threading on skewers.

JAPANESE BEEF WITH BROCCOLI

Serves 4

1 lb beef flank steak

¹/₃ cup soy sauce

¹/₃ cup sake or white wine

¹/₄ tsp instant minced garlic

¹/₄ tsp ground ginger

2 Tbsp cornstarch

¹/₂ bunch fresh broccoli

1 red bell pepper, seeded and sliced

2 green onions with tops, sliced

1 can (8¹/₄-oz) sliced water chestnuts

1 Partially freeze steak and slice thinly across the grain. In a bowl large enough to hold the steak, mix soy sauce, sake or wine, garlic, and ginger. Add steak, cover, and marinate 6 to 24 hours.

2 Stir cornstarch into steak mixture. Place in a 2-qt rectangular glass dish. Cut broccoli into flowerets (see page 150) and save stems for other uses. Add broccoli, bell pepper, green onions, and can of water chestnuts including liquid. Mix well and cover with waxed paper.

3 **MW on high** for 6 minutes. Stir to redistribute ingredients. Re-cover and **MW on high** for 5 to 6 minutes. Serve over steamed rice, page 154.

Pasta And Noodle Meals

Pasta can be cooked in the microwave, but it takes more time than on a conventional stovetop. This is because it takes a long time to boil a large quantity of water in the microwave before adding the pasta. We timed the boiling of 2 qt of tap water. It took 6 minutes on a gas range and 10 minutes for an equal quantity in the microwave.

However, once the water is boiling, and the pasta added, it takes only 6 to 8 minutes on high power to microwave 8 oz of dried pasta, and only half that time to cook fresh pasta.

It's always difficult to cook just the amount of pasta you need. Remember that dried spaghetti quadruples its weight after cooking. A lb of dry pasta will swell to 4 lb, which makes 8 servings. If there's a microwave in the house, you should always plan to cook extra pasta, since cooked spaghetti reheats beautifully! **MW on high** for 1 minute per cup of refrigerated spaghetti, or 2 minutes for the same amount of frozen spaghetti.

BALBOA ISLAND SPAGHETTI

Serves 6

| 1 lb ground beef |
| 1 medium onion, chopped |
| 1 can (28-oz) tomatoes, with liquid |
| 1 can (8-oz) tomato sauce |
| 1 can (6-oz) tomato paste |
| 1 can (4-oz) mushroom pieces, drained |
| 1/3 cup red wine |
| 1/4 cup sliced black olives |
| 2 bay leaves |
| 2 tsp dried basil |
| 1 tsp dried oregano |
| 1/2 tsp instant minced garlic, or 1 clove fresh garlic, minced |
| salt and coarsely ground black pepper to taste |
| 1/2 lb spaghetti, cooked |

1 Crumble ground beef into a dishwasher-safe colander set in a 3- to 4-qt casserole. Sprinkle onion on top. Stirring midway through cooking, **MW on high** for 6 to 7 minutes. Pour grease into an empty can for disposal after it solidifies. Transfer meat to casserole.

2 Drain liquid from tomatoes into casserole. Mash tomatoes coarsely with a fork, or chop in food processor using steel blade. Add tomato sauce, tomato paste, mushrooms, wine, olives, bay leaves, basil, oregano, and garlic. Cover and **MW on high** for 15 minutes, stirring midway through cooking.

3 Stir again, re-cover, and continue to **MW on 30% (medium-low)** for 15 minutes for more blending of flavors. Add salt and pepper to taste. Serve over cooked pasta.

NOTE

This recipe is reprinted from *MicroQuick!*, a microwave cookbook by CiCi Williamson and Ann Steiner.

FISHERMAN'S SPAGHETTI

Serves 4

| 4 Tbsp butter or margarine |
| 1 rib celery, chopped |
| 1 green onion including top, sliced |
| 1 clove garlic, minced |
| 5 Tbsp all-purpose flour |
| 1 can (6½-oz) minced clams, with liquid |
| milk |
| 4 Tbsp (¼ cup) sherry |
| 4 Tbsp (¼ cup) chili sauce |
| salt, black pepper, and cayenne to taste |
| 1 cup peeled and deveined raw shrimp |
| 1 cup crab meat, picked over to remove shell and cartilage |
| ½ lb spaghetti, cooked |

1 Put butter, celery, green onion, and garlic in a 2-qt glass batter bowl. Cover with plastic wrap. **MW on high** for 3 minutes, or until celery is tender. Stir flour into mixture.

2 Drain liquid from clams into a 2-cup glass measure. Set clams aside. Add milk to make 2 cups of liquid. Using a wire whisk, blend liquid into flour mixture. **MW on high** for 3 minutes. Stir with whisk. **MW on high** for 2 to 3 minutes, or until thick.

3 Stir in sherry and chili sauce. Add salt, pepper, and cayenne to taste. Stir in clams, shrimp, and crab meat. **MW on high** for 4 to 5 minutes, or until shrimp are pink and opaque. Serve over cooked spaghetti.

JOHNNY MARZETTI

Serves 6

1 lb ground beef

4 cups uncooked egg noodles

1 Tbsp instant minced onion

¼ tsp garlic powder

¼ tsp black pepper

1½ cups water

1 can (16-oz) sliced stewed tomatoes

1 can (8-oz) tomato sauce

1 cup shredded Cheddar cheese

This is an adaptation of a popular Ohio dish named after Marzetti's restaurant in Columbus.

1 Place a dishwasher-safe plastic colander into a 2-qt casserole dish. **MW on high** for 3 minutes.

2 Use a wooden spoon to stir meat and break up chunks. **MW on high** for 2 minutes, or until meat is no longer pink; stir again. Set colander of meat aside. Pour grease from casserole into a can to discard later.

3 Place noodles in bottom of same dish and distribute meat on top of noodles. Sprinkle onion, garlic powder, and pepper over meat. Pour water, stewed tomatoes, and tomato sauce over top; cover. **MW on high** for 5 minutes.

4 Stir; re-cover. **MW on high** for 5 minutes, and stir again. Re-cover and **MW on high** for 2 to 4 minutes, or until noodles are almost tender. Stir in cheese and let stand 5 minutes before serving.

UNCOOKED NOODLES

Adding uncooked noodles to a casserole of other ingredients eliminates the chore of cooking the noodles separately in a big pot of boiling water. The amount of liquid in a recipe incorporating uncooked noodles has been measured exactly so that the noodles will absorb the proper amount during cooking. Do not substitute ingredients in such a recipe, because doing this may hinder the foods from microwaving correctly.

When adding uncooked noodles to a recipe, make sure they are covered by the other ingredients, so that they will soften and be tender throughout. It is important to stir the ingredients after half of the microwaving time so that the noodles will not stick together as they cook.

LIGHTHEARTED LASAGNE

Serves 6

1 lb ground raw turkey

1 jar (32-oz) spaghetti sauce

½ cup red wine

1 tsp fennel seeds

¼ tsp garlic powder

16 oz cottage cheese

⅓ cup grated Parmesan cheese

½ tsp dried basil

1 Tbsp dried parsley flakes

8 uncooked lasagne noodles

8 oz low-fat Mozzarella cheese, sliced

¼ cup sliced ripe olives

1 Crumble turkey into a 2-qt glass batter bowl. Stir in ½ cup spaghetti sauce. Stirring midway through cooking, **MW on high** for 4 to 5 minutes.

2 Stir sauce again and pour remaining spaghetti sauce into bowl. Pour wine into sauce jar, replace lid, and shake vigorously to loosen remaining sauce in jar. Pour contents of jar into bowl along with fennel seeds and garlic powder. Cover bowl with plastic wrap and **MW on high** for 7 to 8 minutes, or until bubbly.

3 In a small bowl, combine cottage cheese, Parmesan cheese, basil, and parsley; set aside.

4 To assemble lasagne, pour ⅓ of hot spaghetti sauce mixture into a 2-qt rectangular dish; level. Place 3 lasagne noodles in dish, pressing to make contact with sauce. Break off part of another lasagne noodle to fit across end of dish. Spread ½ of cottage cheese mixture on noodles. Arrange half of sliced Mozzarella on top. Pour half of remaining hot spaghetti sauce into dish; level. Repeat layers, with remaining sauce as the final layer. Distribute olives over top.

5 Cover dish with heavy plastic wrap or 2 layers of regular plastic wrap. **MW on high** for 6 minutes, then **MW on 70% (medium-high)** for 20 minutes. Do not remove cover. Let stand 20 to 30 minutes before serving so that noodles can finish cooking.

NOTE

CiCi developed this recipe for the National Turkey Federation in Reston, Virginia. It is high in protein but very low in fat.

Farmer's Market

Vegetables are among the most healthful foods you can eat. It has been proved by scientists at Cornell University that cooking vegetables with microwaves retains more vitamins than any other cooking method. An added bonus is that vegetables are one of the most successful foods to microwave. They develop beautiful, intense colors and the most desirable texture, when cooked according to the directions in this section.

MICROWAVING FROZEN VEGETABLES

The 10-oz waxed-paper-covered boxes of vegetables can be placed directly in the microwave oven. There is no need to remove the paper wrapper, but if your box is covered with an aluminum-foil wrapping, take the foil off. Place the package on a paper towel so the printing ink will not stain the floor of your oven, and **MW on high** for 5 to 6 minutes.

Frozen boxes of spinach and chopped broccoli tend to leak, because they contain more liquid than other frozen vegetables. Stand boxes of spinach and broccoli in a 4-cup glass measure or dish to catch the liquid as the vegetables cook.

To microwave large plastic bags of frozen vegetables, make a 1-in slit in the center of the bag. Place slit side down on a paper towel or plate. Turn bag slit side up after half the cooking, and **MW on high** as follows: for a 16-oz bag, 8 to 10 minutes; for a 20-oz bag, 10 to 12 minutes; for a 24-oz bag, 12 to 14 minutes; for a 32-oz bag, 14 to 16 minutes.

MICROWAVING FRESH VEGETABLES

Do not add water when microwaving most fresh vegetables. For beets, cabbage, carrots, okra, and sliced or diced potatoes, add ½ cup of water per lb of vegetables. Add ¼ cup of water per lb of plain green beans, parsnips, rutabagas, or turnips.

Cover your dish of vegetables with a lid or plastic wrap. If covering the dish with plastic wrap, do not pierce holes in it or turn back a corner of it. Microwaved vegetables will be most tender when the maximum amount of steam has been contained in the dish.

To microwave baking potatoes in their skins, do not put them into a dish or cover them. Pierce each potato once with a fork, and arrange in a circular pattern on a microwave bacon rack.

Microwave vegetables on high, according to the following table:

Vegetable	Minutes Per Pound
Spinach, tomatoes	3 to 4
Corn cut off the cob, parsnips, soft-shelled ("summer") squash,	4 to 5
diced eggplant, okra, peas	5 to 6
Asparagus, broccoli, Brussels sprouts,	6 to 7
cauliflower, baked potatoes, hard-shelled ("winter") squash Cabbage, carrots, green beans, whole new potatoes, sliced or diced potatoes	7 to 10
Whole beets, rutabagas, or turnips	14 to 18

Do not uncover dish at the end of cooking time. Wrap baked potatoes in a terrycloth towel. Let the vegetables stand for half the time it took to microwave them, before serving.

VEGETABLES IN BOILABLE POUCHES

Using a paring knife, make a large X almost from corner to corner through one side of the pouch or bag. Place bag cut side down in a microwave-safe serving dish. **MW on high** for 5 to 6 minutes. To serve, lift the corners of the hot pouch, and contents will empty through the X you cut.

BLANCHING VEGETABLES FOR FREEZING

If you want to blanch fresh vegetables for freezing, microwave them on high power for half the required cooking time. For best results, blanch only 1 lb at a time. Place the trimmed vegetables in freezer-weight ziplocking plastic bags for blanching. The bag can then be set in cold water to chill the vegetables and stop the cooking without getting water on the vegetables.

When the contents have cooled, squeeze the air out of the bag, then seal, label, and freeze. To cook the frozen blanched vegetable, open the bag seal 1 in and place bag in oven. Microwave on high power according to the cooking time for fresh vegetables.

FRESH ARTICHOKES

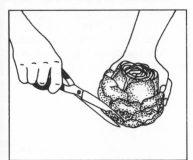

1 Prepare desired number of artichokes by cutting off stems so that artichokes sit flat. Slice ½ in off from tops. Use scissors to cut the thorny tip off each leaf. Wash under cool, running water.

2 Wrap each artichoke in heavy plastic wrap. Turn wrapped artichokes upside down and stand in custard cups or a microwave muffin pan, and place on the floor of microwave oven. If cooking 3 or 4, arrange in triangular or square configuration. **MW on high** for 4 minutes each for 1 or 2 artichokes, and 3 to 3½ minutes each for 3 or 4 artichokes. Midway through cooking, turn each artichoke halfway around.

3 Remove artichokes from oven and sit them on the counter. Use a hot pad to pick up each from its custard cup. Put 1 Tbsp of butter into each hot custard cup, and sit artichoke right-side up on top of cup so that the plastic wrap is not in the butter. Let the artichoke remain on the cup for 10 minutes standing time; the heat from it will melt the butter.

4 When ready to serve, unwrap artichoke and put on a plate with the cup of melted butter. Sprinkle desired seasoning (such as lemon pepper or herbs) into the butter, then dip leaves into seasoned butter.

ASPARAGUS WITH FRENCH MUSTARD SAUCE

Serves 4

1 lb fresh asparagus

2 Tbsp Dijon mustard

3 Tbsp wine vinegar

⅓ cup mayonnaise

salt and black pepper to taste

1 to 2 Tbsp chopped fresh parsley

1 Snap off white portion at bottom of each asparagus spear. Peel especially large or tough spears at the base, using a vegetable peeler. Wash in cool water.

2 Arrange asparagus in a 9 x 5 x 3-in glass loaf pan, with tender tips of asparagus to the center and stems toward the ends of the pan. Cover with plastic wrap and **MW on high** for 6 to 7 minutes. Do not remove plastic wrap. Let stand 3 minutes for carryover cooking to tenderize the asparagus.

3 In a 1-cup glass measure, combine Dijon mustard, vinegar, and mayonnaise. **MW on 70% (medium-high)** for 30 to 40 seconds, or until heated. Do not boil, because mayonnaise will curdle.

4 Drain water from asparagus. Salt and pepper as desired. Pour sauce over asparagus; then sprinkle with parsley.

GREEK GREEN BEANS

Serves 4

1 clove garlic, minced

1 small onion, chopped

¼ cup olive oil

1 lb fresh green beans

1 Tbsp minced fresh parsley

1 tsp fennel seeds

1 tsp dried mint

salt and black pepper to taste

1 Place garlic, onion, and olive oil in a 1-qt casserole. Cover with lid or plastic wrap. **MW on high** for 3 minutes.

2 Put beans in a colander and wash in cool water. Pinch off both ends of beans, and then break in half. Add to onion mixture. Add parsley, fennel seeds,

GREEN VEGETABLES

When people ask us, What does the microwave oven cook best?, we answer, Vegetables! It's reason enough to buy a microwave if you don't have one. Green vegetables remain bright green, they retain more vitamins, and they are tender-crisp when microwaved.

If you prefer the mushy olive-drab green beans Grandma used to cook all day, you may not like the microwave version immediately. Keep trying, and remember that *al dente* vegetables are not only fashionable but also much more healthful.

The most important factor in microwaving fresh green vegetables is the cooking time. This is determined by the weight and type of vegetable. You should have a scale in your kitchen to weigh the food. The weight of the vegetables at the store will not be the weight after trimming or preparation.

mint, salt, and pepper. Stir to coat beans well. Replace lid or plastic wrap and **MW on high** for 6 to 8 minutes. Do not remove cover. Let stand 3 to 5 minutes for carryover cooking to tenderize beans.

TAHITIAN GREEN BEANS

Serves 4

1 package (10-oz) frozen green beans

½ red bell pepper, thinly sliced

1 green onion including top, sliced

1 Tbsp margarine

½ tsp dried basil

1 Place package of frozen beans on a paper towel on floor of oven. **MW on high** for 5 to 6 minutes. Drain water from package; set aside.

2 Place bell pepper, green onion, margarine, and basil in a 1-qt casserole. Cover with casserole lid or plastic wrap. **MW on high** for 2 minutes.

3 Add green beans to casserole and discard package. Re-cover and **MW on high** for 2 minutes, or to desired serving temperature.

BLEU RIBBON BROCCOLI

Serves 4

1 package (10-oz) frozen chopped broccoli

1 Tbsp butter or margarine

1½ oz cream cheese

1 Tbsp all-purpose flour

2 oz bleu cheese, crumbled

½ cup milk

½ can (2.8-oz) French-fried onion rings

1 Place package of frozen broccoli on a paper plate or towel on floor of oven. **MW on high** for 5 to 6 minutes. Squeeze liquid from package and set aside.

2 Place butter and cream cheese in a 4-cup glass measure. **MW on 50% (medium)** for 2 minutes, or until softened. Use a whisk to stir in flour, then bleu cheese. Whisk in milk. Stirring with whisk every minute, **MW on high** for 2 to 3 minutes, or until mixture comes to a boil and thickens.

3 Take broccoli out of packaging and place in a 1-qt casserole. Pour sauce over broccoli and stir to combine. Sprinkle onions over the top. Do not cover. **MW on 70% (medium-high)** for 4 minutes, or until heated through.

BROCCOLI FLOWERETS AND STEMS

To make broccoli "flowerets," place a bunch of broccoli on your cutting board. Using a chef's knife, cut across broccoli, leaving about 2 in of

stems attached to flowered tops. Cut tops into small bunches of bite-size "flowerets."

Save the broccoli stems for other uses. They can be sliced crosswise into coins, to be used raw in tossed salads or on a tray with other vegetables for dips. Broccoli coins can also be microwaved on high for 6 minutes per lb and served as a hot vegetable.

Another way to prepare stems is to grate them, using the shredding blade in a food processor or the large side of a hand grater. They can be used

raw this way in salads, or microwaved in combination with other vegetables.

Broccoli stems can also be cut into pieces and microwaved to serve as a hot, green vegetable. For 2 cups broccoli pieces, place in a 1-qt casserole dish with 2 Tbsp water. Cover with lid or plastic wrap and **MW on high** for 4 to 5 minutes, or until tender. Broccoli pieces are also good in soup.

MUSHROOM BROCCOLI SPEARS

Serves 4

1 lb fresh broccoli

2 Tbsp butter or margarine

¹/₂ tsp instant chicken bouillon granules

¹/₄ tsp dried basil

¹/₄ tsp dried thyme

¹/₄ tsp dry mustard

1 cup sliced fresh mushrooms

1 Cut off tough bottom of broccoli, leaving 4 to 5 in of stem. Slice lengthwise into spears, starting at base of flower and cutting straight down stem. Rinse broccoli in cool water, drain.

2 Arrange broccoli spears in a 2-qt rectangular casserole with stems toward ends of dish and flowers in the center. Cover with plastic wrap. **MW on high** for 6 to 7 minutes. Do not remove plastic wrap. Let stand 3 to 5 minutes for carryover cooking to tenderize broccoli.

3 Place butter in a 2-cup glass measure. **MW on high** for 30 seconds, or until melted. Stir in bouillon, basil, thyme, and dry mustard. Add mushrooms to mixture and stir to coat. Cover with plastic wrap and **MW on high** for 2 minutes. Pour over broccoli.

CAULIFLOWER

An easy way to microwave a head of fresh cauliflower is to cook it whole. Turn the head upside down and cut off the stem close to the base of the cauliflower. Doing this should remove the leaves at the same time. Use a small knife to cut out the core, leaving a cone-shaped hole.

Weigh the cauliflower to determine cooking time. Rinse cauliflower in cool water, and place stem side down in a round baking dish. Cover with plastic wrap. (You may have to use 2 strips if the cauliflower is extra large.)

MW on high for 6 to 7 minutes per lb. Let stand about 3 minutes. Drain water from dish of cooked cauliflower and pour desired sauce over. Sprinkle with paprika.

CONTINENTAL BRUSSELS SPROUTS

Serves 4

1 lb fresh Brussels sprouts

1 Tbsp water

1 tsp instant beef bouillon granules

1 Tbsp butter or margarine

¹/₄ cup grated fresh Parmesan cheese

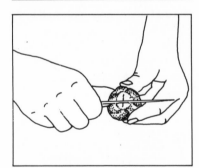

1 To prepare fresh Brussels sprouts, first remove any yellow leaves. Cut off stems and rinse vegetables in cool water. Using a sharp knife, cut an X into stem end of each Brussels sprout.

2 Put prepared Brussels sprouts into a 1-qt round casserole dish. Sprinkle with water and bouillon granules. Cover with lid or plastic wrap and **MW on high** for 5 to 6 minutes.

3 Dot sprouts with butter and stir to combine with cooking liquid. Sprinkle with cheese. Re-cover and let stand about 3 minutes, or until cheese melts.

CORN ON THE COB, OLÉ!

1 to 6 fresh ears of corn

butter

chili powder

salt and black pepper

1 Remove all husks and silk from ears. Rinse in cool water and dry with paper towels.

2 For each ear of corn, tear off a 12-in piece from a roll of heavy plastic wrap. Place 1 ear in the center of each piece of plastic wrap. Butter each ear of corn and sprinkle all rows of kernels lightly with chili powder. Bring sides of plastic wrap together over the ear of corn, and fold it over several times until it is flat against the corn. Twist each end of plastic wrap and tuck under corn. Repeat wrapping other ears of corn.

3 If microwaving 1 or 2 ears of corn, use a dinner plate. Put corn on the plate and **MW on high** for 2¹/₂ to 3 minutes per ear. If microwaving 3 to 6 ears of corn, put them into a 2-qt rectangular glass dish. Exchanging positions of the ears midway through cooking, **MW on high** for 2 to 2¹/₂ minutes per ear. Let stand 5 minutes before unwrapping and serving. Serve with additional butter, and sprinkle with salt and pepper if desired.

NOTE

You can also cut kernels off the cob for cooking in the microwave oven. Put kernels into a casserole dish and cover with lid or plastic wrap. **MW on high** for 2 minutes per cup of corn.

In the frozen vegetable section of the supermarket, you can buy packages of frozen corn on the cob. The corn is packaged in 2 forms: whole ears and "short" ears which are approximately half an ear.

It is not necessary to cook an entire package. Take out the number of ears you want, and put the remainder of the package into a plastic bag. Close bag tightly and return to freezer.

Do not defrost frozen corn on the cob before microwaving. Place the frozen ears in a rectangular dish and cover with plastic wrap. Microwave whole ears on **high** for 3 to 4 minutes each. Microwave "short" ears on **high** for 2 to 2½ minutes each.

EGGPLANT

Past-ripe eggplants can be bitter tasting with soft flesh and tough skins. Size is no indication of quality. A mature eggplant should have a glossy, taut skin and flesh that is just barely resistant to the touch.

A good test is to press down gently on the eggplant with your thumb. If the flesh presses in but bounces back, the eggplant is ripe. If the indentation remains, that means the eggplant is too ripe and the inside may be completely brown with oversize seeds. The eggplant should also feel heavy (light eggplants are pulpy). Choose small or medium-size eggplants because they will have fewer seeds and a firmer

texture than the larger ones. Do not buy an eggplant having soggy areas or brown spots. Store eggplant in a cool place and use within two days of purchase.

EASY EGGPLANT PARMIGIANA

Serves 4

1 small eggplant, about ¾ lb

1 large egg

⅓ cup Italian-seasoned bread crumbs

1½ cups shredded Mozzarella

¼ cup grated Parmesan cheese

1 large ripe tomato, sliced

1 can (8-oz) tomato sauce

1 tsp dried basil

1 Cut stem and green cap off of eggplant. Peel purple skin using a vegetable peeler. Make crosswise slices about ½ in thick.

2 Crack egg into a pie plate and beat lightly with a fork. Place bread crumbs on a square of waxed paper. Dip both sides of eggplant slices in beaten egg and then in crumbs. Arrange in bottom of an 8-in round baking dish, overlapping slices if necessary to fit. Cover with waxed paper. **MW on high** for 8 to 9 minutes, rotating dish a half turn midway through cooking.

3 Sprinkle half of each cheese over eggplant. Place tomato slices on top. Pour tomato sauce over all, and sprinkle with basil. Top with remaining cheese. Re-cover and **MW on 70% (medium-high)** for 6 to 8 minutes. Let stand 5 minutes before serving.

JULIENNE VEGETABLES

To julienne means to cut foods into thin strips the size and shape of matchsticks. Julienned strips of vegetables, meat, poultry, or cheese are used in soups, salads, and many other dishes.

The easiest way to julienne food is to chop it on a wooden cutting board with a chef's knife. First cut the food into 2-in chunks, then cut each chunk in half lengthwise. Continue cutting the chunks until they are in long, thin strips.

CRUNCHY PEAS

Serves 4

1 rib celery, sliced

2 green onions, with tops, sliced

1 Tbsp butter or margarine

4 Tbsp (¼ cup) mayonnaise

¼ tsp ground coriander

salt and black pepper to taste

1 package (10-oz) frozen peas, about 2 cups

½ can (2.8-oz) French-fried onions

Plain frozen peas gain flavor and crunch from celery and 2 kinds of onions.

1 Place celery, green onions, and butter in a 1-qt casserole. Cover with lid or plastic wrap. **MW on high** for 2 minutes.

2 Stir in mayonnaise, coriander, salt, and pepper. Add
frozen peas and stir to break up
frozen chunks. Be sure that mayonnaise mixture and peas are
evenly mixed. Level top of ingredients.

3 Scatter French-fried onions
over top of peas. Do not
cover. **MW on high** for 4 to 5 minutes, or until hot. Serve immediately.

NOTE
Do not microwave assembled casserole until just before serving.
Reheating the mixture may cause
the mayonnaise to curdle. Recipe
may be assembled to the point of
final microwaving up to an hour
before you expect to serve.

NUTMEG SPINACH

Serves 4

1 package (10-oz) frozen chopped spinach

2 Tbsp butter or margarine

1 Tbsp instant minced onion

1/4 to 1/2 tsp ground nutmeg

1/4 tsp sugar

salt and black pepper to taste

1 Stand package of frozen
spinach in a 1-qt casserole
dish. **MW on high** for 5 minutes.
Squeeze box to press out as much
liquid as possible. Discard liquid
in dish. Place spinach in same
dish and discard box.

2 Add butter, onion, nutmeg,
sugar, salt, and pepper. Stir
spinach to mix all ingredients
well. **MW on high** for 2 minutes,
or until heated throughout.

MICROWAVING POTATOES

Who hasn't microwaved a
potato? The best way to
determine microwaving time is
to weigh your potatoes and
multiply by 6 to 7 minutes per
pound on high power.

One curious thing about
microwaving potatoes is that
whole potatoes take less time
to microwave than sliced ones.
This is because the skin holds
in the heat and steam, which
speeds cooking. When slicing
potatoes for a casserole, don't
peel them. Leaving the skin on
takes less preparation time
and is more nutritious.

HAGGERTY

Serves 4

2 Tbsp bacon fat

1 1/2 lb potatoes

1 large onion, thinly sliced

1 cup shredded sharp Cheddar cheese

salt and black pepper

paprika

1 Use half the bacon fat to
grease a 2-qt casserole.
Wash potatoes but do not peel.
Slice potatoes very thin.

2 Fill casserole with alternate
layers of potatoes, onion,
and cheese, sprinkling each layer
with salt and pepper. Top layer of
casserole should be potatoes. Use
remaining bacon fat to dot top
layer of potatoes, then sprinkle
with paprika.

3 Cover dish with lid or plastic wrap and **MW on high**
for 20 to 22 minutes. Let stand 5
minutes before serving.

DOUBLE-CHEESE STUFFED POTATOES

Serves 2

2 medium baking potatoes, about 6 oz each

1 Tbsp butter or margarine

4 Tbsp sour cream

4 Tbsp crumbled bleu cheese

1 Tbsp dried chives

salt and black pepper to taste

2 Tbsp shredded Cheddar cheese

1 Wash potatoes and pierce
one time with a fork. Place
on a microwave meat rack. **MW
on high** 5 1/2 to 6 1/2 minutes.
Cover with a terrycloth towel and
let stand until cool enough to
handle.

2 Slice potatoes in half lengthwise. Leaving shell intact,
scoop cooked potato into a bowl
and chop coarsely. Add margarine, sour cream, bleu cheese,
chives, salt and pepper. Spoon
mixture back into the four shells.
Sprinkle Cheddar cheese on top.
Place on meat rack and do not
cover. **MW on 70% (medium-
high)** for 2 minutes, or to desired
temperature.

NOTE
Tom Keneally, author of
Schindler's List, offers his
variation on baked potatoes. This
is the way Tom fixes them when
guests come to his home in
Australia.

1 Bake potatoes according to
above directions and wrap
in a terrycloth towel. Put a paper
towel on a paper plate or
microwaveable dinner plate.
Arrange 3 strips of bacon on top
and cover with another paper
towel. **MW on high** for 3
minutes, or until crisp; crumble.

2 Slit baked potatoes and top
with a spoonful of sour
cream. Sprinkle crumbled bacon
on top.

GERMAN CARAWAY POTATOES

Serves 4

3 Tbsp butter or margarine

1 Tbsp caraway seeds

1¹/₂ lb small red new potatoes

1 Tbsp red wine vinegar

parsley flakes

salt and black pepper

1 Place butter in a 2-qt casserole. **MW on high** for 30 to 40 seconds, or until melted. Stir in caraway seeds.

2 Scrub potatoes but do not peel. Cut into quarters and stir into butter mixture. Cover with plastic wrap, and **MW on high** for 10 to 12 minutes, stirring midway through cooking.

3 Let dish stand, covered, for 5 minutes. Sprinkle with vinegar and parsley flakes. If desired, add salt and pepper to taste.

HOT TOMATO POTATOES

Serves 4

2 lb potatoes

1 cup water

1 cup dairy sour cream

1 tsp paprika

1 tsp salt

¹/₄ tsp black pepper

3 green onions, with tops, thinly sliced

1 medium tomato, chopped

1 Peel and wash potatoes. Slice ¹/₂ in thick, and cut each slice into 4 chunks. Put potatoes and water into a 2-qt casserole. Cover with lid or plastic wrap. **MW on high** for 8 minutes.

2 Stir potatoes to redistribute chunks. Re-cover and **MW on high** for 8 to 10 minutes, or until tender when pierced with a fork. Do not drain. Stir sour cream, paprika, salt, and pepper into hot potatoes.

3 Place green onions and tomato into a 2-cup glass measure. Cover with plastic wrap and **MW on high** for 2 minutes. Fold into potato mixture. Sprinkle top of casserole with additional paprika. Reheat at serving time using 70% power (medium-high).

BOURBON YAMS

Serves 4

1 can (29-oz) sweet potatoes, drained

2 Tbsp butter or margarine

3 Tbsp orange juice

3 Tbsp bourbon

2 Tbsp packed brown sugar

¹/₄ tsp ground cinnamon

¹/₈ tsp ground nutmeg

pinch of ground cloves

¹/₂ cup chopped pecans

1 Cut potatoes into large pieces and put them in a 1-qt casserole. Set aside.

2 Place butter in a 1-cup glass measure. **MW on high** for 30 seconds, or until melted. Add orange juice, bourbon, brown sugar, cinnamon, nutmeg, and cloves. Stir well and pour mixture over potatoes. Sprinkle with pecans. **MW on high** for 5 to 6 minutes, or until heated throughout.

STEAMED WHITE RICE

Serves 4

2 cups hottest tap water

1 tsp salt

1 cup uncooked long-grain white rice

1 Put water and salt into a 2-qt casserole. Cover with casserole lid or plastic wrap, and **MW on high** for 5 to 6 minutes, or until water is boiling.

2 Using a fork, stir rice into water; re-cover. If your microwave oven has a memory or sequential settings, this is a good time to use them for the following directions. First, **MW on high** for 3 minutes. Next, **MW on 30% (medium-low)** for 12 to 14 minutes. Do not uncover or stir during either stage of cooking.

3 If the rice is done, all water should have been absorbed. Fluff rice with a fork, re-cover, and let stand 5 minutes.

LEFTOVER RICE

It's always a good idea to cook more rice than you need, because leftover rice freezes beautifully. If you freeze rice in microwaveable plastic bags, you can reheat it in the same bag. Frozen cooked rice can be reheated without defrosting first. Open the seal of the bag 1 in for a steam vent, and place the frozen bag of rice into the microwave oven. For each cup of rice, MW on high for 2 minutes. If reheating larger quantities, stir rice midway through estimated cooking time.

Leftover rice can also be refrigerated for 4 to 5 days. One cup of refrigerator-temperature rice will reheat in the microwave oven on high power in about 1 minute.

PEPPER RICE

Serves 4

2 cups hottest tap water

2 Tbsp butter or margarine

2 tsp instant chicken bouillon granules

1/2 red bell pepper, chopped

1/2 green bell pepper, chopped

1 small onion, chopped

1/2 tsp ground turmeric

1/4 tsp ground black pepper

1 cup raw rice

1 Put water and butter in a 2-qt casserole. Cover and **MW on high** for 6 to 7 minutes, or until water boils.

2 Add bouillon to water; stir. Add red and green bell peppers, onion, turmeric, and black pepper. Stir in rice and re-cover. **MW on high** for 4 minutes; then **MW on 30% (medium-low)** for 12 to 13 minutes. Fluff with fork and let stand 5 minutes before serving.

KABULI RICE

Serves 4

2 cups hottest tap water

2 tsp instant chicken bouillon or bouillon cubes

2 Tbsp olive oil

1 cup rice

1 1/2 tsp onion powder

1 tsp lemon pepper

1 tsp ground turmeric

1/4 tsp ground cinnamon

1/4 cup raisins

1/3 cup peanuts

1 Put water, chicken bouillon, and olive oil in a 2-qt casserole. Cover with lid or plastic wrap. **MW on high** for 6 minutes, or until water boils.

2 Stir in rice, onion powder, lemon pepper, turmeric, cinnamon, and raisins. Re-cover and **MW on high** for 4 minutes; then **MW on 30% (medium-low)** for 12 to 14 minutes.

3 Fluff rice with a fork, and add peanuts. Re-cover and let stand 5 minutes before serving.

LONG GRAIN AND WILD RICE

Serves 4

2 1/3 cups hottest tap water

1 package (6-oz) long-grain and wild rice

1 Pour water into a 2-qt casserole dish. Cover with lid or plastic wrap. **MW on high** for 6 minutes, or until water boils.

2 Stir in contents of seasoning packet and rice packet. Re-cover. **MW on high** for 4 minutes; then, **MW on 30% (medium-low)** for 18 to 20 minutes, or until water has been absorbed. Stir with a fork, re-cover, and let stand 5 minutes.

JALAPEÑO CHEESE GRITS

Serves 6

4 cups boiling water

1 cup quick-cooking grits

1/2 tsp salt

4 Tbsp butter or margarine

1 cup shredded Monterey Jack cheese with jalapeños

1 cup shredded sharp Cheddar cheese

2 large eggs

milk

paprika

1 Measure boiling water into a 2-qt glass batter bowl. Gradually stir in grits and salt. Cover with plastic wrap. **MW on high** for 3 minutes; stir. **MW on 50% (medium)** for 4 minutes.

2 Cut butter into chunks, and stir into grits. Stir Jack and Cheddar cheeses into grits until melted.

3 Break eggs into a 1-cup glass measure. Add milk to eggs until mixture measures 1 cup. Stir well into grits.

4 Butter a 2-qt round casserole. Pour grits mixture into casserole and sprinkle with paprika. **MW on 70% (medium-high)** for 8 to 10 minutes. Let stand 5 minutes before serving. Leftovers can be refrigerated or frozen; **MW on 70%** to serving temperature.

WHAT'S A GRIT?

We've never seen one grit without another; they kind of stick together. Grits are ground from dried hominy, but just in case you don't know what hominy is, it is corn that has been puffed, and hulled in a lye solution.

Grits are displayed in the hot cereal section of the supermarket. They can be "regular" or "quick-cooking." For information about how to microwave a single serving of grits, see page 140.

Leftover cooked grits can be reheated in the microwave oven, and also floured and fried conventionally, such as in Eggs Creole, page 99.

More Desserts

If you still have a sweet tooth after seeing the desserts pictured in the front section of this book, here are some different desserts. Most of these pies, brownies, custards, and candies can be microwaved in less than 20 minutes.

BANANA CREAM PIE

Serves 6

4 Tbsp cornstarch

¹⁄₂ cup sugar

¹⁄₈ tsp salt

2¹⁄₄ cups milk

1 large egg

2 tsp vanilla extract

2 medium bananas

9-in pie crust, baked

whipped topping or sweetened whipped cream

1 Combine cornstarch, sugar, and salt in a small bowl. Mix well so that cornstarch won't lump when stirred into milk. Measure milk into a 1-qt glass batter bowl. Using a wire whisk, blend cornstarch mixture into milk. Then add egg, beating well until no egg is visible in mixture.

2 Stirring mixture with whisk every 2 minutes, **MW on high** for 6 to 8 minutes, or until mixture begins to boil. Add vanilla and cool to lukewarm. (If you add sliced bananas to hot pie filling, they will "cook" and make pie watery.)

3 Slice bananas, and stir gently into cooled mixture. Pour into baked pie shell and refrigerate 4 hours or longer.

4 Cover pie with whipped topping. Slice and serve.

RONALD REAGAN'S PUMPKIN PECAN PIE

Serves 6

4 large eggs

2 cups canned or mashed cooked pumpkin

1 cup sugar

¹⁄₂ cup dark corn syrup

1 tsp vanilla extract

¹⁄₂ tsp ground cinnamon

¹⁄₄ tsp salt

9-in pie shell, baked

1 cup chopped pecans

What do a pumpkin and the president of the United States have in common? They both smile a lot in October! If you learn the tricks to microwaving, your treat will be Ronald Reagan's Pumpkin Pecan Pie.

1 Crack eggs into small bowl of electric mixer; beat lightly. Add pumpkin, sugar, corn syrup, vanilla, cinnamon, and salt. Beat on medium speed until smooth. Pour into baked pie shell and top with pecans.

2 Rotating the plate a half turn after 10 minutes of cooking, **MW on 50% (medium)** for 20 to 22 minutes, or until center is set. Let cool before slicing.

PUDDING MIX

To cook any flavor of pudding mix (not instant type), empty the contents of the mix into a 1-qt glass batter bowl. Using a whisk, stir gradually into the pudding mix the amount of milk specified in package directions. Stirring with a whisk every 3 minutes, **MW on high** for 6 minutes if using a 4-serving size package, or 9 minutes if using a 6-serving size package. Pudding has finished cooking when it begins to boil.

Cooked pudding can be poured into a baked pie crust as a pie filling, or poured into individual serving dishes. Cool to lukewarm and refrigerate.

SOUTHERN NUT PIE

Serves 8

1 Tbsp butter or margarine

3 large eggs

½ cup packed light brown sugar

½ cup light corn syrup

½ cup dark corn syrup

1 tsp vanilla extract

¾ cup chopped peanuts

½ cup raisins

9-in pie crust, baked

1 Place butter in a 4-cup glass measure. **MW on high** for 30 seconds, or until melted.

2 Using a whisk, beat in eggs, then sugar, light and dark corn syrups, and vanilla. Stir in peanuts and raisins; pour into baked pie crust.

3 Rotating midway through cooking, **MW on 50% (medium)** for 12 to 15 minutes, or until center is set. Let cool 30 minutes before cutting.

HOMEMADE BROWNIES

Makes 16

⅓ cup butter or margarine

2 squares (1-oz) unsweetened chocolate

1 cup sugar

2 large eggs

¾ cup all-purpose flour

½ tsp baking powder

1 tsp vanilla extract

½ cup chopped pecans

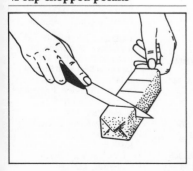

1 Put butter and chocolate in a 2-qt glass batter bowl. **MW on high** for 1½ minutes, or until chocolate is melted.

2 Using a wooden spoon, beat sugar into chocolate mixture. Crack eggs into mixture and beat well. Stir in flour and baking powder until well combined. Stir in vanilla and nuts.

3 Using Crisco or Pam, lightly grease an 8-in square glass baking dish. Pour batter into dish and spread it to a uniform thickness. Turning dish halfway around after 3 minutes, **MW on 70% (medium high)** for 6 to 8 minutes.

OLD-FASHIONED RICE CUSTARD

Serves 4

3 large eggs

⅓ cup sugar

1 tsp vanilla extract

1½ cups milk

½ cup cooked rice

ground nutmeg

1 Crack eggs into a 1-qt round casserole. Beat eggs well, using a fork. Stir in sugar and vanilla. Gradually stir in milk. Stir in rice. Cover with lid or plastic wrap. **MW on 70% (medium-high)** for 4 minutes.

2 Open oven door, reach in and stir mixture with a fork so that it will cook evenly. Re-cover and **MW on 70%** for another 4 minutes.

3 Stir mixture again and then sprinkle nutmeg lightly over top of custard. Re-cover and **MW on 70%** for 2 to 3 minutes, or until mixture jiggles only slightly.

4 Remove cover so that condensing water drops will not drip into the custard during standing time. Let cool at least 15 minutes before serving.

ICE CREAM TOPPINGS

If you haven't tried doing a sauce in your microwave oven yet, you're in for a real treat. Many conventional sauce recipes recommend using a double boiler. However in a microwave oven, a 4-cup glass measure is an ideal cooking utensil because of its shape, handle, and pouring spout.

Along with a measuring cup, we recommend using a stainless-steel wire whisk (available in many sizes) for whisking the sauce smooth. In addition, a rubber scraper will enable you to remove every last bit of your special sauce from the measuring cup.

CHOCOLATE KAHLUA SAUCE

Makes 1½ cups

2 squares (1-oz) semisweet chocolate

1 square (1-oz) unsweetened chocolate

¾ cup half milk and half heavy cream or half and half

3 large egg yolks

½ cup sugar

2 Tbsp Kahlua or coffee liqueur

1 Place chocolate squares in a 1-cup glass measure. **MW on 50% (medium)** for 3½ to 4 minutes. Stir until melted; set aside.

2 Measure milk and cream into a 4-cup glass measure. Whisk in egg yolks until well blended. **MW on 70% (medium-high)** for 3 minutes, whisking every minute.

3 Add sugar; whisk. **MW on 70%** for 1 minute, or until sugar dissolves.

4 Whisk in melted chocolate. Add Kahlua; whisk smooth. Store in refrigerator.

INDEX

TERMINOLOGY AND AVAILABILITY

The names we give ingredients vary from country to country. Here are some selected American terms, with British equivalents.

Baking Items

all-purpose flour is plain flour.
baking soda is bicarbonate of soda.
baking powder is bicarbonate of soda with a pinch of cream of tartar.
cornstarch is cornflour.
sugar is caster sugar unless otherwise indicated.
confectioners sugar is icing sugar.
dark brown sugar is soft brown sugar.
light brown sugar is best substituted with demerara sugar.
light corn syrup is best substituted with golden syrup.
dark corn syrup is closest to light treacle.

Dairy Items

cottage cheese is curd cheese.
cream cheese is full-fat soft cheese.
light cream is single cream.
heavy cream is double cream.
half-and-half is a 50:50 mixture of whole milk and double cream.
sour cream is soured cream.
plain yogurt is natural yoghurt.
whipped topping can be either sweetened whipped cream or whipped nondairy creamer.
butter may be either sweet or salted; most margarines are lightly salted.

Vegetables

beets are beetroot.
Belgian endive is chicory.
chicory is curly endive.
corn is sweetcorn.
eggplant is aubergine.
green onions are spring onions or scallions.
canned pumpkin or pumpkin pie filling can be substituted with pureed cooked hard-shelled squash (add a little sweetening and some cinnamon, nutmeg, and cloves if using as pumpkin pie filling).
snow peas are mangetout peas.

Meats

meats are butchered differently in different countries; substitute the most appropriate cut depending on the preparation involved.
ground beef and other meats are minced meats.
beef flank steak is similar to topside; *shortribs* are cut from under the rib, flat ribs; *cube steaks* are pounded slices from topside or silverside.
lamb is all young spring lamb. *Loin chops* are cutlets from the saddle; *shoulder arm or blade chops* are cutlets from the neck or shoulder.

pork tenderloin is a long, narrow cut from the saddle; *country-style spareribs* are meaty, thick ribs cut from the best end of the saddle.
smoked ham can be either brine- or dry-cured; most recipes for ham use brine-cured, mild and moist ham with a faint smoky aroma, such as boiled ham.
bacon strips or pieces are rashers, usually 1/2 to 1 ounce each. *Canadian bacon* is a long cylindrical cut from the loin that is sugar-cured and smoked.
prosciutto is Parma ham; *country ham* is closest to York ham.

Sauces and Seasonings

condensed soups, such as tomato, mushroom, chicken broth, and so on, are undiluted tinned soups used as a basis for sauces.
brown gravy mix is a dehydrated blend of beef flavoring and seasonings.
taco sauce and enchilada sauce are available in jars or tins in shops carrying Mexican products.
Louisiana Hot Sauce is a bottled sauce similar to Tabasco.
salsa is Mexican hot sauce, either green or red, usually sold in jars in shops carrying Mexican products.
chili sauce is bottled sauce with a tomato base and seasoned with a number of spices.
Thousand Island dressing is a salad dressing made from mayonnaise, chili sauce, green pepper, pimiento, and sometimes chives.
chili powder is a blend of spices, with red pepper (cayenne) as the base.
garlic and onion powder are pulverized dehydrated garlic and onion, available with most other spices and seasonings.
poultry seasoning is a blend of dried herbs, with sage predominating.
onion salt and garlic salt are a blend of garlic or onion powder and salt.
instant minced onion or garlic are dehydrated flakes of either; if unavailable, substitute fresh minced.
Kitchen Bouquet is a bottled concentrate used to darken sauces; substitute minute quantities of Bovril.
meat tenderizer is a commercial powder sprinkled on less tender meats prior to cooking.
Liquid Smoke is a bottled commercial concentrate of smoke flavor, used to give a barbecued flavor to meats.
tomato paste is tomato puree.
cilantro or Chinese parsley is the same as fresh coriander, available in specialty markets.

Starches, Cereals, Breads

quick oats are fast-cooking porridge oats.
hominy grits are the granulated bits of hulled dried maize; available as a cereal.
wild rice is available in gourmet shops; long-grain and wild rice mix is a com-

merical blend with about a 2:1 ratio of white to wild rice.
instant rice is quick-cooking white rice, such as Minute Rice.
dry stuffing mix is a blend of bread cubes, dried herbs, and seasonings; *Italian-flavor* is strongly accented with oregano and basil; *cornbread stuffing* is made with cubes of baked cornbread instead of plain bread.
Bisquick is a commercial baking mix, including flour, fat, bicarbonate of soda, dried milk product, and salt. It yields a scone-type baked product.
flour and corn tortillas are unleavened fried Mexican breads, available in specialty shops featuring Mexican products. Corn tortillas are also sold in cans by El Paso brands.
whole-wheat bread is whole-meal bread.
hero sandwich buns and submarine buns are long, crusty loaves; substitute French breads about 12 inches long.

Desserts, Sweets, Baking

shortening is solid vegetable fat.
cookies are either biscuits or small cakes depending on type.
graham cracker crumbs are crushed graham crackers; substitute any crushed digestive biscuits.
instant coffee powder is instant coffee, such as Nescafe.
lemon cake mix is a commercial preparation, including flour, leavening, fat, and flavorings; substitute your favorite recipe.
lemon pudding mix is a commercial preparation similar to a custard mix.
flaked coconut is desiccated or shredded coconut.
sliced almonds are flaked almonds.
pecans can be substituted with walnuts.
cherry pie filling is a tinned mixture of cherries, sugar, and cornflour thickening, used to fill tarts.
liquid fruit pectin is a commercial powder or liquid used to set homemade preserves.
vanilla or lemon extract is the same as vanilla essence or lemon flavoring.
apple sauce is apple puree.
blueberries can be substituted with bilberries or blackberries.
cocoa is unsweetened; semisweet chocolate is plain chocolate; chocolate morsels are chocolate polka dots.

UTENSILS AND MATERIALS

paper towels are absorbent kitchen towels.
waxed paper is greaseproof paper.
aluminum foil is kitchen foil.

Cookware is measured in either volume or inches. For volume measures, see earlier tables. For inches, use the following:

1/8 inch = 1/2 cm		6 inches = 15 cm	
1/4 inch = 3/4 cm		8 inches = 20 cm	
1/2 inch = 1 1/2 cm		10 inches = 25 cm	
1 inch = 2 1/2 cm		12 inches = 30 cm	